Online Information Services in the Social Sciences

CHANDOS
INFORMATION PROFESSIONAL SERIES

Series Editor: Ruth Rikowski
(email: rikowski@tiscali.co.uk)

Chandos' new series of books are aimed at the busy information professional. They have been specially commissioned to provide the reader with an authoritative view of current thinking. They are designed to provide easy-to-read and (most importantly) practical coverage of topics that are of interest to librarians and other information professionals. If you would like a full listing of current and forthcoming titles, please visit our web site **www.library-chandospublishing.com** or contact Hannah Grace-Williams on email info@chandospublishing.com or telephone number +44 (0) 1865 884447.

New authors: we are always pleased to receive ideas for new titles; if you would like to write a book for Chandos, please contact Dr Glyn Jones on email gjones@chandospublishing.com or telephone number +44 (0) 1865 884447.

Bulk orders: some organisations buy a number of copies of our books. If you are interested in doing this, we would be pleased to discuss a discount. Please contact Hannah Grace-Williams on email info@chandospublishing.com or telephone number +44 (0) 1865 884447.

Online Information Services in the Social Sciences

Edited by

NEIL JACOBS
AND
LESLY HUXLEY

Chandos Publishing
Oxford · England · New Hampshire · USA

Chandos Publishing (Oxford) Limited
Chandos House
5 & 6 Steadys Lane
Stanton Harcourt
Oxford OX29 1RL
UK
Tel: +44 (0) 1865 884447 Fax: +44 (0) 1865 884448
Email: info@chandospublishing.com
www.library-chandospublishing.com

Chandos Publishing USA
3 Front Street, Suite 331
PO Box 338
Rollinsford, NH 03869
USA
Tel: 603 749 9171 Fax: 603 749 6155
Email: BizBks@aol.com

First published in Great Britain in 2004

ISBN:
1 84334 069 0 (paperback)
1 84334 070 4 (hardback)

British Library Cataloguing-in-Publication Data.
A catalogue record for this book is available from the British Library.

Typeset by Concerto, Leighton Buzzard, Bedfordshire, UK (01525 378757)
Printed in the UK and USA

Contents

PART 2 THE INFORMATION ISSUES

PART 3 THE INFORMATION ISSUES

Foreword

The information resources landscape for social sciences has changed radically over the last two decades. Twenty years ago information resources were widely spread and difficult to locate, and their use often limited to specialised researchers requiring specific equipment. Now, the number of information resources has increased, while technological developments such as the Internet and the advance of PCs has made them much more easy to access.

It would be easy to describe the present situation as a paradise for social scientists with all this information at their fingertips to improve the quality of research. It would also be misleading. A recent survey undertaken on behalf of the Research Libraries Support Group[1] in the United Kingdom shows that much remains to be done. Across all disciplines a similar pattern emerged: finding information electronically was deemed relatively easy to do, while accessing the information was more difficult and using it more difficult still.

Taking the process of locating information as an example, the success of the Internet in simplifying this process is easily overestimated. The Internet is clearly a significant tool for researchers and almost half of the social scientists in the above mentioned survey ranked generic search engines such as Google and Yahoo as their second tool for the discovery of information resources, despite their concerns about the quality and provenance of the results. Concerns about the comprehensiveness of such tools did not have a high profile: the whole issue of the invisible or deep Web seems to have not reached the awareness of these social scientists. This is all the more concerning if we take a moment to reflect on the very wide and diverse range of research resources used by the social science community. For example, computerised datasets of primary research data are essential primary sources, and use of these is expected to rise even further. And yet these types of data in particular are not easily retrieved through generic search engines – the very discovery tools of choice, albeit sometimes reluctantly, for many users of social science information!

The lack of awareness shown by the research community of some potentially very useful electronic information resources, such as mediated subject gateways, suggests that advice to researchers on electronic resources needs to be improved, but also, perhaps, that the information services themselves offer scope for further improvement and that their visibility is less than optimal. The authors of this book address these linked issues vividly, comprehensively and with authority, not only describing the more traditional and crucial issues surrounding provision of online services such as functionality and usability, but also incorporating fascinating and valuable accounts of marketing aspects and the development of user skills. Without these, a perfect service might be offered, but its exploitation would in all probability leave much to be desired.

The quality of information services, online or otherwise, depends to a large extent on the depth and breadth of understanding by the developers, contributors and custodians of social science information resources of the needs and behaviour of their various user communities. Information professionals have an important, even crucial, role to play as intermediaries, translators and brokers between their users and the research and development community. It is not only good to see but, more importantly, extremely encouraging and very timely that this book takes an inclusive approach to user communities, including many users outside of the academic environment. With the many advances in technology, increasing numbers of individuals, groups and organisations outside the 'traditional' academic research and learning communities have become more interested and actively involved in using information resources. Moreover, many of these groups will include both actual and potential creators of social science information resources – a simple reflection of the fact that creation, use and re-use are activities which are not the exclusive domains of distinct and mutually exclusive groups. For example, the government and its institutions, clearly (co)creators of many social science information resources, have become more exacting users, looking for research and data with relevance for policy preparation, implementation and review. This environment provides excellent opportunities for developing knowledge transfer activities between the various sectors, in which information services have a crucial supportive role to play.

Information professionals operate within a fascinating, quickly changing and at times confusing landscape of shifting and overlapping user and creator communities, rapid technological changes and a renewed and reinvigorated awareness of the importance of high quality information resources as building blocks for good science, informed decision-making and empowerment of groups and individuals in the modern society. They need to be equipped with the tools and understanding to navigate this landscape and to guide the users of their services to their many destinations.

It is with this in mind that I warmly recommend this book which provides both an outstanding map – charting the social science information landscape with admirable precision – and a reliable compass – by showing us robust and up-to-date methods for setting ourselves and others on an appropriate course.

And, if this is not enough, it also gives intellectual nourishments for more than a few hours of travel.

Drs Astrid Wissenburg
Swindon, January 2004

Note

1. *Researchers' Use of Libraries and other Information Sources: Current Patterns and Future Trends. Final Report.* Education for Change Ltd, SIRU, University of Brighton, The Research Partnership. © HEFCE 2002 *http://www.rslg.ac.uk/research/libuse/.*

About the contributors

This book is the product of experience gained on projects and services run at the Institute for Learning and Research Technology (ILRT) at the University of Bristol. At the time of writing, all the contributors worked at ILRT.

The ILRT is able to daw on a wide range of skills and expertise to offer advice and consultancy concerning online information resources to organisations in the education, government, voluntary and commercial sectors. Further information is available from the ILRT website at *http://www.ilrt.bris.ac.uk/*.

Sarah Agarwal is a Project Manager for the Internet Development Consultancy, based at the ILRT. She specialises in user-centred design and business analysis.

Paul Ayres is Senior Cataloguer on Regard, the online research service of the UK Economic and Social Research Council (ESRC). His interests include communicating academic research so it is accessible to non-specialists.

Grace de la Flor works in the user experience phase of web application development. This involves gathering user requirements, conducting usability tests and developing information flow.

Ale Fernandez is a Web Developer, specialising in development methodologies and in the use of open source software in the voluntary sector.

Debra Hiom is the Director of the Social Science Information Gateway (SOSIG) and a unit leader on the MSc in Information and Library Management at the University of Bristol. Her research interests include resource discovery and digital libraries.

Lesly Huxley is Research Director and one of two Assistant Directors of ILRT and University of Bristol Information Services. She has been involved in several national and European digital library projects and services and has research interests in organisational and people development.

Neil Jacobs is Manager of Regard, the online research service of the ESRC. He also teaches on the MSc in Education, Technology and Society at the University of Bristol. His research interests include digital libraries and discourse analysis.

Angela Joyce is a Research Officer for the Social Science Information Gateway (SOSIG). Her background is in modern languages and information management; special interests are non-English Internet communities and European Union developments.

Claire Lumber is the Technical Developer of Regard, the online research service of the ESRC. Her skills are in relational databases and Internet development.

Christine Mullings is Survey Officer for Regard, the online research service of the ESRC. Her research activities have included work-related information needs and use in many different organisations.

Andy Ramsden is a Learning Technology Adviser at the University of Bristol. Within this capacity is his interest in designing and developing accessible e-learning material.

Paul Shabajee is a Research Fellow at the ILRT. His research interests include the design and use of web-based technologies in education.

Sue Timmis is Director of Regard, the online research service of the ESRC. Her research interests include information-seeking behaviours and the evaluation of innovations. Sue has been a consultant to a wide range of education, commercial and voluntary sector organisations.

Helen Wharam is a chartered librarian who has worked at the BBC and currently works for Resource Guide for Social Sciences, a service to support learning, teaching and research in higher education. She also teaches on the MSc in Information and Library Management at the University of Bristol.

The authors may be contacted as follows:

Institute for Learning and Research Technology
University of Bristol
8–10 Berkeley Square
BRISTOL
BS8 1HH
UK

Tel: +44 (0)117 928 7193
Fax: +44 (0)117 928 7112
E-mail: ilrt@bristol.ac.uk

1

Introduction

Neil Jacobs

It has become a commonplace to say that we live in a knowledge economy or an information society. Tony Blair has said that 'it is likely that the Internet in time will become as ubiquitous as electricity is today' (BBC, 2000). This is also the Prime Minister of a UK government that has consciously adopted the mantra of 'evidence-informed policy', or 'what matters is what works'. Evidence about precisely what does work, when and why has always been important across all sectors of society, for policy-makers, practitioners, journalists and researchers. The Internet now offers us the chance to find out quickly and effectively, but all too often this potential is wasted when those looking for evidence merely type a keyword into a search engine such as *Google*[1] and assume that the results they get are all (or even the best) that is available. When those results run to more than one page, there is also the temptation to assume that the first ten hits are as good as any, and that this is the evidence base upon which decisions can be made. The costs of this kind of poor match between user needs, skills and service are incalculable, both in financial terms and in terms of quality of life.

And yet it needn't be like this. For years, librarians have quietly assured those who would listen that more, better evidence can be derived from properly managed resources, queried by knowledgeable professionals with a clear view of both the research question and the capabilities of the system. As library budgets continue to suffer real-terms cuts, now is perhaps a good time to demonstrate the many ways in which information professionals are making services more effective and relevant, and building the capacity of those that use them.

The challenge, though, is daunting. Sandra Nutley and Huw Davies have noted that 'social science knowledge is necessarily imprecise, inconclusive, complex and contingent, whereas policymakers and practitioners, it is argued, can only use knowledge if it is precise, gives clear guidance, and is formulated in sufficiently simple terms to be directly applied' (Nutley and Davies, 2000). If the knowledge itself needs configuring to be useful, then many of the resources that deliver that knowledge are small, incomplete and inconsistent. As Maurice Line (ex Director General, Science, Technology and Industry at the British Library) puts it, 'almost any social scientist has to search at least three or four [services] to obtain reasonable coverage of a topic. Very few of them do, of course, partly because it is too much trouble, partly because they do not think it matters much if they miss something' (Line, 2000). There are some important tools that are going to help in terms of being able to bring together otherwise disparate information, but much of the work is going to be organisational and cultural: translating the knowledge from one context into another without losing anything important in the translation, synthesising it and persuading users to use it.

But this is to get ahead of ourselves. This book is written to help those information professionals who find themselves offering services to users of social science information. What do I mean by 'social science information'? The intellectual scale of the social sciences is vast, covering the micro-sociology of conversation analysts and ethnomethodologists, the arcane mathematical modelling in econometrics, studies of international relations with a historical range, social psychological investigations, major panel surveys and so on. The scope of social science information is equally vast, covering large quantitative datasets, research reports, policy papers, books, legal documents, substantive and methodological guidelines, video data, journal articles, working papers, and so on. If the information is varied, then the uses it may be put to are diverse in the extreme. Social science information is clearly relevant in the academic world, but it is also relevant to government, local government and government agencies, to the voluntary and community sectors, to the commercial sector (market researchers, consultancies, financial corporations), to trade unions, and to those in all branches of the media with the unenviable task of translating between these worlds. Finally, information is now global, and so the scope of the book is not limited to the UK, but also considers the international context, including cultural and linguistic issues.

Information resources should be developed to meet the needs of these users, which are embedded in their practices (what they do) and in the context of their working lives. That is, people's needs for information do not arise in the abstract but arise from their work, i.e. are practical tasks that have success criteria, deadlines and so on. These tasks usually involve bringing together several types of material, of which social science information is only one among many. It is a premise of this book that without knowing about these practices, the information professional will not be able to offer any added value to them and will fade into irrelevance. However, by bringing together knowledge of people's practices and needs, skills relating to information tools and technologies, and insight into what is shaping the future, the information professional should find him or herself invaluable. This book has been written to help make information professionals invaluable, to help us identify opportunities and really exploit them to the benefit of our organisations and our profession.

Part 1 of the book describes a number of case studies (the style of which varies both with their subject and their author) from the UK and beyond. Its objective is to give the reader a taste of what users do, why they do it, and why they do it in the ways they do. It does not represent extensive market research, although later chapters do draw on available research into user needs. It is not comprehensive, but illustrative. It is intended to surprise readers with the sheer range of tasks for which social science information is used and the diversity of contexts in which social science information is relevant. Why would this be important? It is important because surprise is a good basis on which to reassess our knowledge of the range of topics that information professionals like to think of as our core work. Key themes that emerge from the case studies (discussed further in Chapter 12) include the value of quick, effective retrieval such as offered by Google, the importance of personalisation, the range of barriers to information, and the bases upon which people make judgements about the relevance and reliability of information. When these issues are projected onto the work of information professionals, they cast new light on some traditional concerns, such as selection and metadata, topics that information professionals are discovering, such as marketing, and topics that are assuming greater relevance in the online world, such as usability and accessibility.

Clearly, there is a vast wealth of knowledge on all of these topics, and it would be ridiculous for this book to try to encapsulate that within its limited scope. Instead, Part 2 offers practical insights from people working in these areas about how to bring together theoretical knowledge with insight into user needs in order to run an online information service that does add value, and run it effectively and efficiently.

Finally, Part 3 offers a 'heads-up', a scan of the horizon to identify the major social, organisational and technical trends that information professionals should be aware of if they are going to orient their service to exploit the new opportunities. Here, the book takes some advantage of its domain, social science, to outline how social scientists have characterised the 'information society', before looking in more detail at the technologies that will be relevant to the work of information professionals in the next five to ten years. The book ends with an assessment of what all this means for the evolving role of information professionals. We argue that the range of opportunities facing the profession is wide, but that they need to be seized. For example, developments commonly labelled 'technological', such as the development of ontologies, are often continuations (under a new guise) of long-established work in information science. Practitioners and service managers need to be engaged in this work, as we seek to enhance our organisations and our profession, and avoid the irony of an information society without information professionals.

Note

1. I should make clear that I am a great fan of Google. Indeed, I know people who only came back to the Internet because Google enabled them to find the resources they needed, quickly and effectively. However, it is not the best resource for much serious social science information.

   Note that throughout the text addresses of references in italics may be found in the Links section at the end of the book.

Part 1
The case studies

Nine of the following ten chapters in this part describe the experiences of people, mostly end-users, who interact with online information services in the social sciences. Each case study is based on an in-depth interview with that person, undertaken during 2003. Many of them have had their own and their organisation's names changed to enable them to speak more candidly than they would have been able to otherwise. Chapter 12 draws some lessons from the case studies and looks forward to the rest of the book.

2

The trade union researcher: Sandeep

Neil Jacobs

Note: The name of the researcher and details of the union he works for have been changed to preserve anonymity.

Background

Trade unions have very particular research needs, which arise from their members' needs. We might characterise a trade union as being a mediating institution located between government and the citizen, and its members' needs reflect this dual orientation. On the one hand, trade union members are looking for better pay, better health and safety conditions, more job security and so on. Union officials who are working to provide these benefits need sector intelligence to make an effective case. On the other hand, government policies seek to direct the labour market in particular ways and trade unions need to respond to such policies. Of course, the need for research may also come from outside this relationship, from what Harold Macmillan famously described as 'events, dear boy, events', from unforeseen opportunities and threats that emerge in the wider environment.

Sandeep works for the APU, which is the major trade union representing legal sector workers in the UK. APU reached this position after a series of mergers with other unions and Sandeep has stayed with the union throughout, cementing his place as a key member of the union's research staff. These staff, like the union's other 200 employees, are based both centrally in London and (like Sandeep) at the union's regional offices. In fact, Sandeep works mainly from home these days. He graduated with a Masters in social history and a PhD in the history of science some six years ago and has been using the Internet to support his research since then. In fact, the initial prompt for his Internet use was the launch of the *British Library Catalogue* online, saving him countless trips from York where he was a student. We can see, then, that Sandeep's career reflects the increasing mobility of information, with him increasingly being able to choose his location without regard to where information is 'held'.

Practice

The research work in the APU is split both according to institution (such as particular major law firms) and theme (such as health and safety). Each researcher will have a portfolio of a number of institutions and a number of themes on which they lead and about which they may be asked to provide information. Sandeep has a number of regular jobs that need to be done every month, will participate in longer-term research projects and is certain to get some ad hoc requests for reports on particular issues with very short deadlines. This case study will focus on these three types of practice.

Every month, Sandeep produces a pay bargaining report for union negotiators. This report tells them about the major economic trends that they need to be aware of, both generally (such as the retail price index) and in the legal sector in particular (such as recent settlements). The information has to be accurate, and it has to be easily digested. A wide variety of people (pay negotiators, other union researchers, union representatives and so on) will need to read the report and will rely on its contents to inform their activities.

In terms of discrete, longer-term projects, Sandeep will be asked by the union to look at a particular issue perhaps in relation to a new government or European Union (EU) policy proposal. Unions will usually respond in consultation exercises of this kind, either individually or through mediating bodies such as the UK trade union Congress (TUC). For example, with the APU's general secretary on a government task force on UK and European regulation, Sandeep might be asked to produce a report for him on exemptions to employment law across a number of *OECD* countries.

Things crop up. In 2003, a disease called SARS (severe acute respiratory syndrome) spread across the world, claiming hundreds, perhaps thousands, of victims. Members of the APU union contacted Sandeep for advice on all kinds of implications of the SARS epidemic and so he produced a concise report for them, summarising official advice. The timescale for this report was one day because the epidemic was moving quickly and its consequences were mounting equally quickly.

Using information

The information requirements for regular and short-term reports are, in fact, fairly similar. The information needs to be up to date, clear, accurate and (most importantly) authoritative. This similarity in information need is largely due to the audience for Sandeep's work in these two types of case, which is the union's members in all their diversity. As a mediating institution, a union has a duty to disseminate relevant information to its members about the wider world that they can then use in their work.

For both the regular and short-term reports, Sandeep uses a well-established, but different, set of information sources. He uses these because they are the authoritative sources in their particular domains, and this suggests that 'branding', in the deep sense of having an established offline reputation before providing an online service (Braunstein and Levine 2000), is a key requirement for an information source that Sandeep will find useful for these tasks. His regular pay bargaining reports draw from the *Income Data Services* (IDS) *Report*, *IRS Employment Review* and Bargaining Report (now incorporated into Workplace Report), produced by the *Labour Research Department*. For the most part, Sandeep relies on his own subscriptions to these periodicals and uses the paper versions rather than the online services. The one exception is the online indexes to these publications, which Sandeep uses to answer ad hoc queries:

> So there's the virtual online indexes to both those periodicals, IDS and IRS, that I do tend to use much more frequently, because that's updated monthly and so if somebody rings up with a query about working time, or they want the most recent information about working time, then I can do a search of those indexes, and they will tell me where the articles are.

Sandeep will then go to his paper archive (he keeps 18 months of back runs of each periodical; anything before that would not get used), rather than to the online versions, even though his subscription includes access to the online versions. The main online source he does use for the pay bargaining report is the UK *National Statistics* website (for retail price index and labour market figures) which he accesses via the press release page each month. He may also use the *BBCi* site for information about house prices.

As well as external resources, Sandeep also builds his own database of pay settlements and scales relevant to the industries in which he works. He builds this from a variety of sources and finds the resulting resource more useful (at least, he uses it more) than, for example, the *IDS PayBenchmark* database. The latter appears to be too general for his work. Furthermore, the act of building his own resource ensures that he keeps up with his contacts within the industry.

While the pay bargaining report is a regular event with predictable information requirements, ad hoc queries such as the SARS report are by their very nature both less predictable and more urgent. For this reason, only online sources are generally accessible and up to date enough. However, the need for authority is just as high. Sandeep was not being asked for his view, or even the APU's view, on SARS-related questions, but for a summary of the official guidance: 'I didn't want to have anything that was speculative'. For this, he naturally went to the websites of the *UK Public Health Laboratory Service* and the *Health and Safety*

Executive. He specifically did not use news stories, though he was certainly aware of these. He did, however, use a number of relevant FAQs to get background information on the disease, its incidence and origins.

There were overriding and clear criteria for the SARS information, just as there were for the pay bargaining report, which led fairly inevitably to the choice of sources to use. This is less true of longer-term research projects, such as the comparative analysis of exemptions to employment law mentioned above. Because such information is not collated systematically at an international level (indeed, this was part of the project), it was not clear at the start where to find the answers. Sandeep used three starting points: the primary legislation, individual trade union contacts and the Web. Much primary legislation is now available on the Web and this enabled Sandeep to gain a quick overview of the policy framework within each country he was covering. However, to get a clearer view of the way things worked on the ground, and the issues behind that, he first used the major union websites, such as *AFL-CIO* for the United States and *ETUC* for Europe. His next step was decided by language. Because he is not sufficiently fluent in Italian, Sandeep did not use the websites of the Italian unions or other industry bodies, but instead called known contacts in some of these organisations. Only rarely might he 'cold call' a number from a website: 'I wouldn't just pick somebody's name off a site and ring them'. In contrast, his research on exemptions to employment law in the US was conducted largely using the websites of organisations such as the *US Small Business Administration*, links for which were found on the *AFL-CIO* site. Language, then, remains a factor in the Web's potential for conducting research. The Web has other drawbacks as an information source. For example, Sandeep conducted a review of comparable directors' pay, drawing on the annual reports of various companies as found on their websites. Sandeep found that each site was structured differently, often poorly (as if designed by people with more interest in image than substance), so that it was difficult and time-consuming to find the information he was looking for.

Information services

Although Sandeep does occasionally use the union's library service, it is a long way from being central to his job. For the most part, he is self-reliant: selecting, building and managing his own collections of reports and periodicals and his own database of pay settlements and scales. Even where he needs to go beyond his own resources, he has sufficient skills and networks to be able to uncover the information he needs. We are faced with a user who has an apparently limited call for a dedicated information service.

However, we can see that when he steps beyond his own resources and his more predictable tasks, Sandeep finds information resources less tailored to his needs. Sometimes this will be inevitable: it is unlikely that the legal and social contexts of countries will ever be sufficiently similar to support the operation of an 'employment law exemptions' portal. However, where information is available in relatively standard formats, such as company accounts, then services may exist that could help. For example, in the UK the official *Companies House* site offers company accounts for a small fee. Alternatively, the reports of listed companies in Europe and the US are available for free from, for example, *CAROL*.

Sometimes, of course, such services do not exist. For example, should Sandeep need to review the research and policy analysis done by UK unions into a particular health and safety issue, then (as he did looking for directors' pay) he would have to visit a series of differently organised websites and work out on each where such information might be found. Clearly, there is scope here for online information services to review what users such as Sandeep do and organise information accordingly (within the constraints of having to maintain the distinct identity of individual organisations). This is a matter of metadata, of being as consistent as possible with mark-up formats and record structures.

So much for the technology, what about the user? Sandeep is not only building his resources and collections independently, but also his skills:

> I probably wouldn't say I've had any particular training, no. It's a bit like even with the Microsoft suite of stuff, you know, I've not had any particular training in that really, but I use it every day, therefore it becomes tacit knowledge really. You get to know it by using it constantly.

However, while it is true to say that training without practice is of limited use, this does not necessarily mean that practice without training is any more valuable. Sandeep is both experienced and highly qualified (having a PhD), but his use of online sources is limited to simple keyword searches and accessing the sites of organisations known from the 'real' world. He does not use potentially useful databases of research evidence, perhaps because this is not expected or because they may cost money, but also perhaps because they are unfamiliar and their potential is unrecognised.

Sandeep has, pretty much, built his own personal information environment. He is at home in a familiar information ecology that has its problems without being overwhelmingly problematic. Certainly, there are ways in which online information services could improve his environment, some of which he recognises. However, information workers should beware of too quickly carving out a niche for themselves. Many of the practices that Sandeep engages in and that from an 'information' perspective might be improved in fact serve other purposes too. As I mentioned above, building his own database of pay settlements may seem like additional work, but in fact it does keep Sandeep engaged with the people who use his reports. And user engagement, as any information worker will tell you, is key to providing a successful service.

3

The further education lecturer: Peter

Debra Hiom

Note: The views expressed are those of the lecturer concerned, not necessarily of the employing organisation.

Background

> By 2010, 90% of young people by age 22 will have participated in a full time programme fitting them for entry into higher education or skilled employment. (Department for Education and Skills, 2001)

The above target is taken from the 2001 Education and Skills report from the UK Department for Education and Skills (DfES) and clearly places further education (FE) high on the government's agenda. There have been a number of high-profile initiatives such as *UfI* and *LearnDirect*. In April 2001 the *Learning and Skills Council* (LSC) was launched taking over from the former Training and Enterprise Councils and the Further Education Funding Council in England. The LSC's remit is to plan and fund all post-16 education through FE colleges, school sixth forms, work-based training for young people, workforce development, adult and community learning, information, advice and guidance for adults, and education–business links. The FE sector in the UK is therefore quite a different beast to higher education: in addition to having approximately three times the number of students it also differs enormously in the number of qualifications, the range of courses and the types of learners and their capabilities. This places a different emphasis on the information needs of FE.

Peter works in a large FE college with over 35,000 students (many of whom are part-time learners) distributed across a number of campuses. He is the subject team leader in sociology (with over 20 years' experience) and a faculty IT champion. It should be said at the outset that Peter is perhaps not typical of FE lecturers and there are still not a huge number of people using information and communications technology (ICT) in their learning and teaching. Even Peter is not as advanced in his use of ICT resources as he would like to be and still doesn't have an opportunity to fully use them in the classroom.

Using information

Peter makes wide use of information and the process of gathering, analysing, interpreting and disseminating this to others is fundamental to his role as a college lecturer. He is also a heavy user of the Internet. Again this is mostly for gathering information at the moment as there is no access to the Internet in a classroom setting (although he hopes this will change next term when it is planned to have a data projector and laptop with Internet access for use in classes). In the meantime he will often set tasks based around utilisation of the Internet for the whole class (in the dedicated IT lounge) or occasionally for individual students. He is confident in his use of the Internet and has created a website and teaching materials that he uses to support his work. He also makes heavy use of e-mail and word processing.

Each site in the college has an LRC (learning resource centre) but Peter doesn't tend to make use of it very much nowadays. This is mostly because he believes the emphasis of teaching has shifted: it is less knowledge based and more about stimulating learning for which more up-to-date material is available from the Internet. He still makes use of the LRC for reading certain journals such as the *Sociology Review* but generally doesn't need to visit the centre on a regular basis.

Peter has recently created two Level 3 sociology modules for use within the *National Learning Network* (NLN). The project involved providing text and ideas for learning objects of 20 minutes of student material for each module. A template for the material was provided which restricted the amount of text that could be put into each screen. The brief that Peter was given was that the modules should be as interactive as possible and aim to have different material to that which the student could find from a textbook. The project was completed to extremely tight timescales and required material to be very contemporary (something you don't typically find in textbooks).

Peter found the Internet to be an ideal source for this project and virtually the entire information gathering was done online. He mostly relied on *Google* to find sites and resources and also made heavy use of the Guardian's online service, *Guardian Unlimited*, for news stories on topics such as the World Trade Center, the Spanner Case, Iraq, etc. He then linked information he found via the Internet to current standard sociology texts. Generally he is always looking for new and current topics so that students can relate to the information more easily.

Typically he separates his browsing and gathering of information from the analysis. While working on the sociology modules he would go to Google and save seven or eight sources into a folder in his favourites directory, which he would return to later to see if they were of use.

He sometimes will find material by knowing the name of another sociologist: 'bang in their name and find their site'. However you need to know who's who to do this. Perhaps because of the pace and pressure of the FE sector he doesn't tend to use colleagues as a source of information as people 'tend to plough their own furrows'.

Peter doesn't have particular concerns about the quality of the material as he is often looking for stimulus material for students so it doesn't necessarily have to be academically sound in order for it to be useful. Generally Peter relies on his experience in the field to know whether information is correct or not. He doesn't regularly check sources as it is so time consuming (and isn't sure he would know how to go about it anyway).

In general Peter is happy with his experiences of finding and using information online, although sometimes he would like to be able to ask for information in a different way: 'Keywords on a website can differ so much that is hard to know just what to ask for sometimes.'

Future needs

Peter believes that lecturers in FE need to forget about producing notes and handouts as these can easily be bought elsewhere. Instead, they need to concentrate on:

> ... interesting things to do with the information – this is a way to claw back creativity into teaching.

Peter feels that he is starting to use technology to make it more useful for learning and teaching. He can begin to tailor lessons to provide more difficult pieces of text knowing that only some students will use them, but making it more interesting for those students. However, time is an obstacle, and lots of this work is still done on an individual basis and often from home, which may cause a barrier for other staff to be involved. Peter finds that there is still generally 'institutional inertia' to getting ICT really integrated into the FE curriculum despite the huge central push to try and make this happen.

4

The voluntary organisation: Wendy

Sue Timmis

Note: The views expressed here are those of the individual concerned and not necessarily of the employing organisation.

Background

Wendy Stephenson is Deputy Director of *Voscur*, a Bristol-based voluntary sector umbrella body. Their website describes their remit as follows:

> Voscur is a support agency for the community and voluntary sector in Bristol. Our membership now includes over 470 local groups, covering a wide range of activities. Voscur is a member-led organisation, and we act as a network of community and voluntary groups working with the public and private sector to regenerate Bristol.

Voscur employs ten staff and became core-funded by Bristol City Council a year ago. At this point the Deputy Director role was created and Wendy is the first person to hold this post. Voscur has two main objectives: to provide support and information for its voluntary and community organisation membership (and others) and to support representatives from the community and voluntary sector to participate in different strategic partnerships and the democratic process in Bristol. They also run a number of additional projects with a variety of funding streams.

Voscur provides information to its members in a variety of ways: a monthly newsletter, a website and a weekly e-bulletin. There are also funder-finder sessions, where Voscur supports members in using the funder-finder database to look for funding from different trusts. They also have a library that members can use.

Prior to joining Voscur a year ago, Wendy worked for 13 years for another voluntary sector initiative called the *Sofa Project* concerned with furniture recycling. Prior to that she was involved in a youth training scheme in Bristol, so has been employed in the community and voluntary sector most of her working life. She is therefore very familiar with the needs of this sector and Voscur members in particular.

Practice

Wendy's role has both an internal and external focus and she works with information in many of the functions within her job. She oversees the operational management of the organisation and line manages several of the staff. However, she also works with the four geographical membership networks and some external bodies such as an organisation called the South West Forum, which is a regional umbrella body for local umbrella bodies. Wendy is on their business management committee. In addition to this, all staff at Voscur have an information-seeking and processing role:

> Part of their job is to filter information so we all feed into the newsletter that our information worker produces. Each of us is allocated different publications to look through. Each of us extracts information that is relevant to our membership so all of us have that role within the organisation.

Wendy is a confident ICT user who regularly utilises the Internet and e-mail in her work, although her use of the Internet is more limited at work than it is at home and she does not feel that her usage has increased over the last year. Although she had some training in how to use e-mail originally, she has never had any Internet training. While she feels confident that she can achieve the results she wants and needs, this is counterbalanced by a feeling that she could achieve more or be more efficient in her searching behaviour if only she knew more:

> I've just picked it up. I did buy a book once but found that more difficult than doing it myself. So when I search I'm sure there are formulae I could use but I don't because I don't know how to. So a lot of it is guesswork I think.
>
> ... but I usually get the information that I want in the end, but perhaps I could get there quicker if I was more competent in using the facilities. I don't know because we don't have anything to compare it with or know how competent others are.

In approaching a specific information-seeking task Wendy develops a clear plan, building in a variety of strategies drawn from her existing networks and regular information sources. An example of this concerned researching information on national 'compacts'. Voscur has been involved in developing a compact with the local authority and other statutory bodies in Bristol. A compact is an agreement on how bodies work together and it sets out the consultative and funding arrangements for example. This is a national initiative and there is a national compact and complementary local compacts. Wendy was asked to develop part of the Bristol Compact and needed to undertake some research into consultative processes as part of this:

> My starting point for that was to think, well, this must have been done before so where can I find that information? So I looked at the government's website and found examples that other people had got together which varied enormously from two sides of A4 to 25-page documents. So I took a random selection of different compacts based on nothing more than what I might have known about the city where that compact had been developed. I looked at a few online and then downloaded a selection and printed some off and started looking through and taking the best elements out of the different compacts. I looked at the Bristol City Council website because I know they have some guidelines on consultation so I printed those off and then I went and met the person at BCC who's written those and we spoke about how they could be changed or improved and what our input into that would be.

Wendy found the UK government website that contains details of compacts from one of the regular newsletters that they subscribe to. She had also done some training around consultation and looked at the notes from this and, through responses to a consultation that Voscur had carried out with its members, extracted comments on the consultation. Although online information was important in this search strategy, it was only one of several sources and all of the sources were derived from existing contacts. The source of the information is very important for voluntary sector organisations such as Voscur and Wendy affirmed that they look to the national bodies for a lead on most of the information that they both need and disseminate.

Wendy felt that this was a successful information-seeking task where the process was quite straightforward. The most positive aspect of this for her was being able to look at other people's work and the commitments that other areas have made. This is potentially of great value in both the public and voluntary sectors where the culture of collaboration and sharing is more developed than in some other sectors. However, the range of information and the different styles of compact meant quite a lot of sifting and qualitative assessment. Wendy felt that some sort of ranking or guidance in assessing the quality of material and the identification of models of good practice would have helped her in this task, although this would have been likely to involve an evaluative process and therefore not strictly be the concern of information providers.

Using information

Most of the information Wendy makes use of comes from regular newsletters and e-bulletins, e.g. the *NCVO* (National Council for Voluntary Organisations), the *NACVS* (National Association of Councils for Voluntary Service), the *Pro-funding* bulletin, *VolResource* magazine, *Regeneration and Renewal* magazine and *New Start* magazine.

Wendy scans about three e-bulletins a week and uses more online services than others in her organisation. Her reasons for this were:

> Part of my job is managing the information worker so I am ultimately responsible for the newsletter and information that we send out, so I feel I must look at those e-bulletins.

This strong motivation seems to indicate that the e-bulletins are seen as providing more current or more targeted information than the paper-based newsletters. The importance of national bodies as disseminators of information was mentioned earlier in this chapter. Wendy also emphasised their importance when discussing information overload and the problems of duplication of effort. The way that information is received by Voscur is quite random; this makes them quite dependent on the national bodies to feed them with appropriate information and could be construed as encouraging passivity. However, Wendy felt that this was a good thing:

> I think it's good that it comes from them because they do the first job of making it accessible to us and then we make it accessible to our members.

Accessibility of the language and content are very important for Wendy in online information and these requirements were reiterated in later discussion. When describing the most important thing she was looking for, Wendy emphasised accessibility again:

> Accessible language I think, clear indexing – so anything that was going to help my search really and I wanted a variety of examples that I could select from.

When investigating compacts, Wendy searched the government website using the site search facilities, which is her regular habit as she finds following links can be frustrating: 'Often you follow links and don't get where you think you are going to get.' She had not used this site before and there were some issues in locating, filtering and measuring the quality of information. Wendy's expectations were that the information would be very obvious and she would not have to hunt for it.

> I expected the government website to be reliable and the information would be easy to access. I think as I recall it wasn't quite clear from the home page where I was going to go to so I did spend a bit of time looking. I remember that now and I was looking for something which I thought was straightforward which was examples of other compacts but it wasn't immediately clear where they were but I did find them – perhaps I was being too fussy!

The expectations of ease of use and information on demand together with the complexity and amount of information are increasing all the time, and this appears to be leading to dissatisfaction and frustration over the behaviour required to achieve results.

Future needs

When considering how services might develop in the future, Wendy again mentioned instructions and making better use of the resources through guidance:

> I don't think there are instructions with search engines on how to use search engines – so perhaps that would be helpful if they were right there in front of you.

Voscur would also like to develop their website to include more interactive services for their members such as newsgroups, but Wendy commented that a major obstacle for them is that there is no channel of communication for discovering new ICT-related opportunities:

> I suppose because I don't keep up with what might be happening in the world of IT then I don't know what opportunities there might be...

> ... I suppose we get our IT support from a local company who does things like help us set up our LAN and sort our problems which are few and far between, touch wood! And we had someone who designed and set up our website but we don't really have anyone who's feeding us information about opportunities. We all use our computers as tools ... we are not really that IT motivated or interested in the latest gadgets: we are not gadget driven so perhaps we don't hear about things.

This is a key issue for voluntary sector organisations which generally receive lower levels of ICT support than other sectors, especially small organisations such as Voscur. For these organisations, information issues need to be seen as an integral part of ICT strategy, and opportunities for finding out more about suitable opportunities afforded by technology without focusing on 'gadgets' seem to be essential. Given the strong emphasis on working with national bodies, it may be that the information resource providers should consider collaboration with such bodies to deliver these opportunities.

5

The academic: Sandra

Christine Mullings

Note: The name of the academic and details of the organisation she works for have been changed to preserve anonymity.

Background

Dr Sandra Latham works in a department based within a medical faculty and is involved with teaching, administration and research activities.

Using information

Sandra uses information in all sorts of ways linked to her varied activities, from gathering it and analysing it to providing it to others. She uses Internet resources a lot, 'about a hundred times a day', but does not rely solely on these sources. She also uses library books and hard-copy journals and talks to or asks people for information. She is very familiar with and practised in using other ICT skills and mentioned using Explorer, Mulberry e-mail client, Word, Excel and PowerPoint nearly everyday, as well as using Photoshop, Reference Manager and SPSS sometimes. Word is the main software package that she uses.

Sandra uses quite a mixture of resources. She is a confident Internet user, though she felt that there were probably more resources out there that she did not know about. She uses the Internet in three main ways: first, to look for contact data – finding people or where they are located, or their e-mail address;

second, to look for specific data, for instance key statistics such as population denominator statistics, or for reports and papers. For these she refers to specific websites such as *National Statistics*, the World Health Organisation (*WHO*), the United Nations (*UN*), the *European Science Foundation* and various US and UK government websites. The third way she uses the Internet is very exploratory and linked to her research on any specific topic or topics as detailed in the case study she talked about, which was writing a couple of chapters for an undergraduate textbook. Topics researched in this way include health in Cuba, the industrial revolution, the history of acupuncture, anthrax and the plague, suicide and many others. Some sites she used because she found they were good for that topic, such as the *BBC* for educational information. Although primarily aimed at children, she found the *BBC* sites to be a reliable starting point. On the whole her searching was serendipitous, using a general search engine (usually Google) and starting with a keyword or topic and going on from there following the links as they appealed to her. 'I just click around, I do it very quickly.'

When asked about her feelings regarding her use of information, whether she thought the sources she found would be reliable, Sandra was astute in assessing their worth. She felt that the quality of the site could be gauged quite quickly, partly by the presentation of the website and partly by the style of writing: 'You get a gut feeling about the quality.' If she did not feel that the source was good or the data reliable, she would try and verify it by looking at sites that were more academic. On the whole she was looking for balanced information, but not entirely:

> Sometimes if you are looking for a particular extreme view on a topic that is very judgemental, that can also be useful, to show the range of views on a topic.

Information services

Her department has a library and Sandra uses it mainly to collect information from statistical volumes and to browse paper copies of journals as she feels it is easier to browse through the hard copy. She uses the library catalogue and online databases frequently and she tends to use and search electronic journals rather than ask the librarian (who is part time). In addition to her departmental library she also uses the main university medical library or occasionally the social sciences library. She has not had any particular training in searching for or using online information recently, only some training on software use in the past. She often receives e-mails about various new online resources but rarely has time to check them out, unless they are directly relevant to what she is currently working on.

For Sandra, the best aspect of using online sources of information is the speed and variety of things 'you would never have found – it would have taken a long time to find all the interesting bits and pieces on paper'. One of the worst aspects of the Internet in Sandra's view is trying to remember where you saw something, or using some information and forgetting to note down where it came from, or the link no longer being there when you go back so you can't cite it. She felt that because of the volume of information she is looking at and because she can look at so many things so quickly, she might see something and afterwards think that it would be useful but not remember where she saw it. The way she dealt with this was to try and guess her search terms. Although she does bookmark some of her favourite sites, she felt that she had got too many, 'like a big one called "Health" which is just so big now'.

Sandra related that publishers discourage academics from using too many web sources and restricted these to reliable key ones because of the problem of not being able to get hold of the source. Her final comment was:

> I think the Internet is great for academic work and other things as well. For the case study, I could have sat here and looked at all sorts of things, all sorts of different information. But the Internet has changed our expectations that things get done instantly, the volume of what is expected, to do more work. You're supposed to be able to access everything and do it yesterday.

6

The media consultant: Jeremy

Neil Jacobs

Note: The names of the consultant and various clients have been changed to preserve anonymity.

Background

Media work can be the hardest to support. Deadlines are short, and the people working in the media are usually experienced and talented information workers in their own right. This is certainly the case with Jeremy.

Jeremy is a freelance media writer and consultant, living in Southampton but working across the UK and worldwide. His work is all about getting the message of social science research to journalists and to government policy-makers. To do this he works with central government, with research funders, with journalists and with academic researchers. People in these various walks of life do not always have the same concerns, the same sensitivities or goals, or even speak the same language. However, it is vital that they communicate effectively if we are to have public policy informed by the rigorous research that goes on in universities. Jeremy is a key figure ensuring that this happens to the extent that it does, at least in the UK.

Jeremy spent his early career working for a major publisher, which gave him the chance to build the principal information resource that he uses in his work, his network of contacts. As he says:

> Everyone says they'll work for themselves and be a millionaire by the time they're 35 these days. But I say, 'you can't just go

> out and work for yourself as soon as you leave university, you know, you need something, whatever it is, to go to. And one way to do that is to get a large organisation to employ you that will pay for you to travel widely and meet loads of people, and build a network from which you'll build your career.'

About ten years ago, Jeremy started working more intensively as a journalist, writer and consultant, which are the ways he describes himself today.

Practice

Jeremy does many things. As he says, 'there are so many different things that I do, and some of them are very short term – working on a press release or a short article for some kind of publication'. This makes it difficult to think about his practice in general. However, we could say that Jeremy concentrates on four main activities. He writes books (though less often than he used to), he is commissioned to write reports of research, he writes articles and he helps academic researchers communicate with the outside world about their work. The thing that links all these things is that they are 'all about trying to help social scientists to communicate in one form or another!'

Typically, perhaps, someone will approach Jeremy and ask him to put together a report, or perhaps bring together the relevant experts, to summarise the key points in a particular subject. This would be like the best part of writing a book, the initial planning and scoping out of the project, investigating a field and developing a view of it. So, for example, a research funder might be interested in seeing whether it would be sensible to fund a programme of research into poverty and personal finances: how do poor people manage their money? They would want to get a view of this topic from both senior researchers and policy-makers. Jeremy's role here would be to gather together these people with sufficient skill that they are able to talk to each other easily and effectively. Often, when researchers try to communicate with people outside universities, they find it difficult and can soon alienate the very people they are trying to communicate with. There are many reasons for this, but Jeremy finds his niche in overcoming these problems and ensuring that social policy really can be informed by the evidence from academic research.

This may sound simple; it is anything but. For example, what counts as a coherent summary of research in a particular field? An academic might answer that a coherent summary is one where the theory and concepts all fit together. A policy-maker might insist that a coherent summary is one that relates to existing policies and institutions. A conventional journalist may reply that a coherent summary is one that relates to the issues that people find important in the real world. Jeremy has a different view to all of these. I asked Jeremy whether he thought that sociology was the same as economics in having a coherent set of concepts (the academic view of coherence). He answered that:

> Perhaps sociology doesn't fit together. I think some sociologists would say that, that I know. Lots of people call themselves sociologists, but they would barely be able to talk to each other, they do such different things...

In this revealing quote, Jeremy shows that coherence to him is a matter of communication rather than concepts or headlines, of people being able to talk to one another. This is the skill and practice that defines his work.

Using information

You could say that Jeremy has two ways of thinking about information. Firstly, there is what information professionals call 'current awareness'. This awareness needs to be not only of the areas of research that he covers, but also what users of that research are thinking (policy-makers, journalists, the general public) and furthermore he needs to be aware of new resources and tools available to help him in his information gathering. Secondly, there is the overview of a research or policy area that I touched on above and will say more about below. Given these intensive information needs, I asked Jeremy whether he used libraries: 'No. Do I use any libraries at all? Only what I've got at home and the Internet. Very, very rarely do I use libraries.' This may seem like proof of what many information professionals have feared for some time, that their role is disappearing. However, this is not so, as will become clear.

Current awareness

In terms of what I have called 'current awareness', Jeremy reads *The Economist* and *The Financial Times*. He may also read some issues of other UK newspapers such as the *Guardian*, *The Observer* and *The Sunday Times*, other UK magazines such as *The New Statesman*, and American newspapers and magazines (notably *The New York Times* and the *New Yorker*). While he does all of this on paper, he also makes use of online versions such as *Economist.com*. Ironically, given the concern of many information professionals that online material is not being properly archived, Jeremy uses sites like *Economist.com* as an archive: 'These days there's Economist.com so I can go and find stuff again when I need it.'

Jeremy's other main medium for current awareness is regular e-mail digests. He receives these weekly from media organisations (such as *Guardian Unlimited*), research organisations (such as the *Institute of Development Studies*) and think-tanks such as the Johnson Russia List from the US *Center for Defense Information*. Of course, all of these resources are developed and put together by information experts, whether or not they call themselves this.

This mix of sources not only keeps Jeremy informed about current research output, but also keeps him in the loop of what he calls the 'national or international conversation' – both the producer and the user sides of social research. To keep up to date about emerging tools to help him, such as 'the whole blogging phenomenon', Jeremy finds the technology sections of both the *FT* and *The Economist* more than adequate.

Overview

So we come back to the issue touched on above: what is an 'overview' of a topic, and how is it achieved? In one sense, a topic's overview is defined by the media objects that host it. While resources such as *The Economist* magazine are 'functional', in that they enable Jeremy to keep up to date with developments in his field, they also work at a deeper level to define that field and to help Jeremy control his information gathering. As he says, 'I have this idea that there are certain things that you have to read and if you've read those then you know as much as you need to.' In another sense, a topic's overview is something to be worked up as appropriate on each occasion (for example, the gathering of experts and policy-makers mentioned above). In this second sense, an overview is the result of a negotiation that Jeremy manages between the producers of research and its (potential) users. This may be a matter of using his network of contacts, or it may be a matter of using his skill and experience to make a piece of research address an issue of importance outside the academic world. As he says:

> The kind of stuff I'm doing now... it's fitting [research] into the agenda of the public (if they have an agenda), the government, what companies are interested in, and reflecting what the media agenda is... So what I do when I'm taking a piece of research that's done by a scholar which has some relation to policy or some relation to some issue in the news, is try to make that connection.

The 'overview' he needs here is an overview of the policy or media agenda into which he can position a new fact or finding. Of course, Jeremy gets part of this overview from his current awareness activities, discussed above.

Finally, things are different if Jeremy is, for example, writing a book. In this case developing an overview of the topic is not so much a matter of sticking to a particular media source or of negotiation, but the more traditional kind of comprehensive information searching and synthesis. In fact, Jeremy does little of this kind of work these days, preferring to stick with shorter-term projects that allow him to exploit his contacts, his up-to-date information and his skills at making connections. This is also a matter of control and avoiding information overload. Being freelance, Jeremy needs to be able to predict and control his workload, something that can be difficult on longer-term projects. As he says:

> I tend to focus on projects where I can pretty much know how much time it will take, or I bill the client on the basis of the time taken. Because if you're writing a book... you can research something to death... you are never quite confident that you've completely covered the area.

Ad hoc information needs

Things crop up. Jeremy may be asked by a journalist to recommend an expert in a field he is less familiar with, or he may need quickly to find key reports on a particular topic. For these needs, Jeremy is aware of and will use more traditional information sources. For example, in finding experts, he may turn to the ESRC's database *Regard*. In locating key reports, he may look for a classified subject gateway such as *SOSIG*:

> I think the best websites are those, the ones where everything is cleverly layered and... maybe you drill down to find what you want.

However, these activities and resources are not at the heart of his practice.

Information services

So what does all this mean for information services? Those that Jeremy uses, such as e-mail digests, appear to him to be largely automated. His principal sources of information are discrete media entities such as *The Economist*, and his network of contacts. Furthermore, he is as skilled at accessing, synthesising and adding value to information as anyone calling themselves an 'information professional'. However, all this is not as bleak as it might appear for those seeking to offer online information services. For one thing, Jeremy does occasionally use more traditional online services such as web gateways and databases. More importantly, though, Jeremy challenges information professionals to make his life easier by, for example, making it less complicated for him to get an overview of ongoing national and international debates on particular topics. Software is available to create useful digests of stories appearing across media outlets, but Jeremy does not yet find this useful enough to rely on. He is looking for explicit and trustworthy selection and editorial policies, such as those of the paper issues of *The Economist* and the *Guardian*. The online versions of both are too exhaustive for browsing or current awareness: they do not work as definitions of a topic or area in the way that their offline counterparts do. There may not be opportunities to present Jeremy with a comprehensive 'personal information environment' (HeadLine, 1999, *Subject Portals Project*), because the relevant overview shifts from task to task and from occasion to occasion. Nevertheless, the core sources remain, and might form the basis of a personalised current awareness service. In many ways, Jeremy is the archetypal knowledge economy worker (see Chapter 23); he is mobile and highly skilled, and he exploits and adds value to technical knowledge, putting it to use to improve the efficiency and effectiveness of societal processes such as policy-making. He is, perhaps, a 'hard case' for information services to support. But a service finding a role in his activities will be securely at the heart of today's economy.

7

An international student: Olaf

Debra Hiom

Note: The views expressed here are those of the individual concerned and not necessarily of his organisation.

Background

Olaf is a first-year PhD student in the Social and Political Science Department of the *European University Institute* (EUI) in Florence, Italy. The EUI was founded in 1972 by the then European member states to promote European research. There are over 300 research students enrolled at any one time from all countries in the European Union and beyond. Typically, students will be proficient in more than one European language and seminars can officially be held in multiple languages.

Practice

Olaf is Polish. Prior to enrolling on the EUI doctoral programme he had studied both in Poland and the Netherlands. More recently Olaf has been working as a research fellow in a Warsaw-based think-tank dealing with European security issues. He intends to combine his PhD with his job and writes articles for the Polish press from time to time. His PhD research topic is on Polish political culture and its impact upon Polish foreign security policy up to 1989 and especially whether historical experiences affect Polish thinking about international politics and international relations.

Using information

As a new PhD student, Olaf is taking a number of taught courses. One is a compulsory module on comparative methodologies but others are dependent on the student's interests. In addition to this taught element, he is concentrating on gathering information on his research topic. While he is making some use of the library for this, most of the information gathering is being done through the Web:

> ... I mean it's more convenient for me to search on the Web because, you know, I have no time now to read everything so I'm just collecting many articles and saving them on my hard disk, in PDF ... So what I'm basically doing is ... I'm building up my own private archive.

He is concentrating mainly on collecting journal articles at this point in his research but again prefers to use the Web rather than going to the library to gain access to these:

> I mean searching them on the Web is basically more useful [than the library]... if I have a choice between printed journals and electronic journals I would prefer electronic journals ... just simply when I search information, because when I read I prefer printed journals.

He tends to focus on a handful of academic journals published by well-known professors or by leading institutes that he depends upon for information, such as *International Affairs* and the *Journal of Common Market Studies*. In order to expand his search further he often turns to Google for information, although he admits that in order to use Google and other such services effectively you have to know what you are looking for in order to confine the search. Olaf's previous work experience in international relations stands him in good stead for assessing the results returned through search engines:

> If I know that there is a professor in my discipline who's well known, well his name is for instance Copperfield, ... so I put

> 'Copperfield' and then I see [the results]. But it requires for me a basic knowledge about the subject.

He makes some use of pre-print articles and working papers but uses them mostly to look at the way in which ideas are being approached and developed by other researchers and so tends to view these more as methodological training materials rather than as secondary source material for his research topic:

> Working papers are usually written by people like me, so not very big names really... basically it's a formula for student researchers so you can see how people develop their concepts.

He also needs to collect primary material for his research, including texts of debates in parliament, minutes of commissions, and so on. The Polish parliament has quite a good website and provides access to commissioned bulletins and to parliamentary debates for the last ten years. But it's available almost exclusively in Polish (apart from some summaries in English) so he needs to translate the documents.

Another major source of information for Olaf is recommendations from the university and from colleagues in his previous job. He also makes some use of alerting services but tries to restrict the number of services he uses to two or three to avoid information overload.

The way Olaf uses information has changed over time: a few years ago he would print out or copy information he found but nowadays he tends to save files on his laptop and every month or so will go through the folders and try to decide which ones are useful for his research and which ones can be deleted. He is also looking ahead to the time when he returns to Poland and won't have access to such a wide range of online journals so is collecting them for use in three to five years' time.

> Because when you deal with certain subjects for five years then you know which articles are not worth saving: they're written but nobody reads them and they will disappear, and you know which articles are let's say classical articles, so basic articles to which you know everyone is referring to in his or her PhD or other pamphlets.

His difficulties with using information are mainly technical: he has a problem with accessing some e-journals because they need a special browser or plug-in software. He also sometimes has problems viewing special character sets such as Polish or German as you need to change the browser in order to view them properly.

Future needs

Olaf's view of the Web is that it is currently fairly chaotic but at the same time democratic, in that anyone can make information available to the wider world. He also recognises that students increasingly have to be more independent in terms of their research and can no longer depend on their supervisor to direct them so closely:

> You know there are a lot of people, students, PhD candidates who are doing their research on their own. Okay they have a supervisor who they meet like once a month or once twice a year and basically they are supposed to write their PhD on their own actually. Because I mean in practice you know one professor has you know like 100 PhD candidates, I mean it's impossible to manage.

In order to help this situation he has a strong view that the Web needs to be much more structured and rigorous and sees the possibility of web services providing direction for researchers, almost becoming 'quasi-supervisors' for their work:

> Especially in political sciences and social sciences there are all these complicated and very sophisticated theories. You've got to know what is the beginning, what is the source and what [work] has been built upon this basic theory. So I would expect the Web or basically the services to be less democratic, more sort of giving you advice.

Acknowledgement

The research on which this chapter is based was carried out at the European University Institute Library (Florence) under the auspices of EUSSIRF, part of the the European Commission's Access to Research Infrastrucures section within the Fifth Framework Programme (Improving Human Research Potential).

The Cochrane Library: Jo and Ioannis

Helen Wharam

Note: The views expressed here are those of the individuals concerned and not necessarily of their employing organisations.

Background

The *Cochrane Library* is an electronic publication designed to supply high-quality evidence to inform people providing and receiving health care and those responsible for research, teaching, funding and administration at all levels. It contains the most comprehensive and international collection of evidence on which interventions have been shown to work and which need more research. The *Cochrane Library* is considered to be the best single source of reliable evidence about the effects of health care. It is internationally regarded as providing the gold standard in 'what works and what does not' and is used by researchers and clinicians worldwide and increasingly by patients and their families. The *Cochrane Collaboration*, the *NHS Centre for Reviews and Dissemination* and other bodies compile the Library, which is published by John Wiley.

The *Cochrane Library* is freely available to NHS staff, patients and the public in England through the *National Electronic Library for Health* (NeLH).

Published on a quarterly basis and made available both on CD-ROM and the Internet, the *Cochrane Library* consists of a regularly updated collection of eight databases which provide information for those looking for 'the best current evidence', including the *Cochrane Database of Systematic Reviews* which holds protocols and regularly updated evidence-based systematic reviews prepared by the *Cochrane Collaboration*. The aim of those writing systematic reviews is to look at every trial that has ever taken place on a particular intervention; empirical studies demonstrate that Cochrane reviews are more likely to be more methodologically rigorous than reviews published in major medical journals.

Over 50 groups produce these reviews, generally on medical conditions, but also on others such as psychiatric and psychological conditions. Each group has an editorial base with a trials search coordinator who does the searching, a review group coordinator who is an administrator, a coordinating editor and an international and often multidisciplinary panel of editors. Some do this work on a voluntary basis. Reviews can be quite technical, though a clear abstract is provided and a consumer network writes 'tabloid version' reviews specifically aimed at patients.

The *Cochrane Library* offers full-text searching as well as keyword searching and the software allows users to edit and save search strategies, download records and print easily. Feedback and comments from users on both the content and the product are encouraged.

Using information

Jo Abbott has a Masters degree in information and library management and has worked for two years as a trials search coordinator for the Cochrane Developmental, Psychosocial and Learning Problems Group, based at the School for Policy Studies in the University of Bristol. The group has been going for about five years and there has been a Trials Search Coordinator for three years. This group looks mainly at problems in children and would include subjects ranging from bedwetting to sleep disorders to autism, although other topics, from domestic violence to sexual offending, are also examined. The reviewers include paediatricians, child psychologists and social workers.

Approximately 50 per cent are based in the UK, the others come from other countries; Jo's role is to help them all. On average, it may take a reviewer two years from first approaching the group to getting a review published. One such reviewer is Dr Ioannis Kakavelakis, a Research Associate also based in Bristol at the School for Policy Studies. Part of his contract is to do a review for the *Cochrane Library*. For this he received training in the specific approach required from the Cochrane headquarters in Oxford. He has published his protocol (Kakavelakis and Macdonald, 2003) and is now in the process of writing his review. This involves synthesising the information to identify the effectiveness of an intervention, that is whether or not a particular intervention makes a difference, by comparing the intervention against a control group not using the intervention. Publishing a review in the *Cochrane Library* will be good for his professional standing and the training received encouraged him to become very focused, detailed and systematic in his approach.

The reviewer develops a specific question, which for Ioannis's current review concerns the provision of training for foster carers. In this case, he needed to identify which population(s) to investigate, for example mother and father, single parent or gay couple. Once the specific question is chosen, the reviewer and search coordinator between them have to attempt to collect all the available information on the subject, whether it's published or not regardless of language, avoiding bias, that is, whether the findings support or contradict each other, and including unpublished material such as theses. Studies not showing significant results are often not published, but results will therefore be skewed if these are not also traced and included.

Jo and Ioannis work closely together at this stage in the process. It is Jo's role to gather the information and her specialist skills in setting up the search strategy are very important in capturing every possible combination of terms. She may have time to remove any item she spots which appears wildly inappropriate, but it is the role of the reviewer to analyse the information once it has been retrieved. If her post were full time, she might be able to play a greater part in assessing the relevance of material, but because of the very wide scope of her group the search strategies retrieve a wide range of records so she feels that assessment is best done by subject specialists. At the same time, Ioannis acknowledges how valuable it is to have dedicated staff on hand with whom to discuss the search strategies.

Databases searched to inform Ioannis's protocol included:

- Cochrane Controlled Trials Register (*CCTR*);
- MEDLINE (provided through the US *PubMed* service);
- *EMBASE* (a service of publishers Elsevier);
- the Cumulative Index to Nursing and Allied Health Literature (*CINAHL*);
- Healthstar (available through *PubMed*);
- *PsychINFO*;
- Applied Social Sciences Index and Abstracts (ASSIA) provided by *Cambridge Scientific Abstracts*;
- LILACS (available via *BIREME*, the Latin American and Caribbean Health Information Center);
- Educational Resources Information Centre (*ERIC*);
- Sociofile;
- *National Research Register*.

These and others used cannot really be ranked since, as Ioannis says, all are useful when the aim is to be all-inclusive.

Jo is highly experienced at using electronic resources. Most of her searching is done on specific electronic databases, though she does occasionally search the Web. She cannot search every resource that she is asked to as she is limited by what the University of Bristol has access to. In these instances she writes a search strategy for the reviewer who then can normally perform their own search. This is often the way forward with reviewers from overseas wishing to search databases that are specific to that country.

Jo observes that reviewers' needs and skills vary widely. Some have never done any electronic searching and want her to do it all for them. All are doing their reviews on a voluntary basis and the process requires a big commitment in terms of time, usually to be fitted in around full-time jobs by working in evenings and at weekends, so a lot of goodwill is needed and she is eager to help as much as possible. Jo likes to think that the reviewers do get something out of the process, by learning some of the steps involved. She is keen to provide training if it is sought and described a case of a newly-retired person who had never used electronic databases or the Internet, but who was really interested in learning and wanted to do all her own searching for her recently published review. Jo tends to provide training on devising search strategies and searching electronic databases, plus showing reviewers how to find specialist material such as grey literature.

Ioannis is an experienced user of Internet resources, finding *Google* particularly useful. He also looks at sites such as the *British Association of Adoption and Fostering* and the *Child Welfare League of America.*

Although he made heavy use of his university library when studying for his PhD and comments that he is very fond of libraries, he acknowledges that frustration can set in, for instance if the required materials are lost, hidden or not stocked. Nowadays he mainly uses his desktop for accessing information, particularly as Jo and her colleagues identify which journals are available electronically. He also searches non-electronic databases and hand-searches journals to make sure nothing is missed. All potential sources must be checked. Initially he starts by browsing, then uses keyword searches.

The protocol is sent outside the group for comments through a peer review process. Ioannis also works closely with his co-reviewer Professor Geraldine Macdonald, who suggested further terms that he and Jo could search.

For Ioannis, the best part of the process is feeling secure in the knowledge that every item has been found. The most difficult part of the process is ensuring quality while having very little time to go through the retrieved information. As he says, some topics can result in 2,000 papers or other sources of information! Interestingly, he has no expectations about the outcome of the searches, having 'learned not to'. Doing this in his spare time, his motivation comes from being genuinely interested in his subject and wanting to communicate with the community. He and Jo have ensured that all the safeguards are in place to produce a good piece of work and while he observes that it is perhaps not highly original, its strength is that it's systematic. The implications of such reviews can potentially be quite massive; he hopes that policy-makers, clinicians and social workers may use his review to inform decision-making.

This particular group has a very wide scope, so there are practical problems in terms of the sheer numbers of databases to be searched for each reviewer. Jo usually searches between six and ten databases individually for each review, so it's an enormously time-consuming process. Some of the databases vary in terms of functionality and some only have basic search facilities, which is a problem for Jo as she is doing fairly complex searches. Ideally, all should enable advanced searches, plus other facilities such as the ability to edit and delete, and so on.

In terms of language or cultural issues, this international collaboration does not experience problems. The reviews must be published in English, so reviewers' language skills tend to be good. There are no language restrictions in terms of searching, but Jo points out that, as a predominantly medical organisation, they can feel relatively confident that much of the material is available on the major English language databases such as MEDLINE. However she does regularly search in English, Spanish and Portuguese on a Latin American database called LILACS (via *BIREME*), with help from a colleague who translates the search strategies. Being a worldwide organisation that encourages collaboration, there is a big informal translation network available to her.

There is no parity among the groups regarding access to resources. The university or hospital where each group is based determines this. Financially there are restrictions on what Jo can access; groups based in London have the advantage of being able to use the British Library. Jo has taken the opportunity to search for grey literature at the British Library when she has been in London on training courses. Her group cannot afford to pay the British Library to perform searches. Whether or not there may be a time when all the resources she needs are available on the Internet may depend upon the providers and whether they need to make a profit. She points out that some resources can already be accessed freely. For instance, some of her colleagues in other groups use MEDLINE and EMBASE which are freely available through *PubMed*, but the search mechanisms are less sophisticated so Jo is lucky that Bristol University subscribes to access them through *Ovid*.

Both Jo and Ioannis acknowledge issues in trying to deal with such large amounts of information. As Ioannis says, 'time is the biggest obstacle' and 'as work increases there are not enough hours in the day'.

Ioannis would like more to be available on the Internet and both say that being able to access journals electronically helps a lot, as PDF files can be downloaded straight to the desktop. More electronic journals would make a big difference. Funding can be an issue: some groups have greater funding, so are able to obtain more hard copies for their reviewers.

Future needs

The quality of reviews performed for the *Cochrane Library* is paramount. This is in conflict with lack of time to identify the ever-increasing amounts of information produced. Methods to help collect information more efficiently would be beneficial. This could include parity among database search functions. Internet availability of more, reliable, resources would also assist. Funding parity between the different groups would also help, so that all groups could access the required materials through the best possible hosts.

9

The legal viewpoint: Annabel

Paul Ayres

Note: The names of the information manager and the organisation have been changed to preserve anonymity.

Background

The legal profession is reliant on timely, accurate and above all authoritative information in order to give advice to clients. As a user of social science information, many of the key sources are well established and a well-stocked library is an essential component of any large law firm. However, such information units have undergone massive change in recent years in terms of the information they hold or provide access to and the role they play within these organisations.

Annabel worked as the information manager at a leading law firm for almost five years. While a trained information professional, her insights into the key role an information service plays in the legal process show that distinguishing a user from a provider of information is increasingly difficult:

> It was a very interesting five years to be there, at the start of the period we didn't have our own PCs and I can't imagine how we coped as Internet-based resources were just beginning to be used ... by the time I left most things were Web based and much of it on subscription.

This change in the nature of information provision produced many consequences, including the increased need for training in information-seeking behaviour (for professionals as well as users), a massive increase in the speed with which information is handled and a rise in expectations from both users and information professionals about what electronic sources can provide.

Practice

A key role played by the information unit was as an enquiry service. This varied work included three main strands: providing the original and current wording of Acts of Parliament, Statutory Instruments or other legislation; providing access to case law and case materials (as English law is partly based on how legislation is interpreted in specific cases); and the largest proportion of the work, which related to acquiring company information for corporate cases and commercial work.

While this gives the impression of being a very passive information-searching and providing role, it is nothing of the sort. Each enquiry that comes to the library is based on a case where a fee-earning lawyer is seeking to give advice to a client. This means that behind each enquiry is a much broader story which the librarian must find out about using reference enquiry techniques, then analyse the available sources and provide information, answers or materials as appropriate.

The ability to prioritise is vital in handling an enquiry and one of the most important things to find out is who is asking the question as this will shape the response. Time and urgency are also crucial factors, meaning that research for an ongoing case will come after finding a piece of information required to make a decision on a corporate deal that may be going through that day. Being in the commercial world means that money is a part of the process so that any fee-based services, like buying a report or searching a charged-for-by-the minute database, will need to be cleared by the client or the lawyer acting on their behalf before they are used.

Using information

Annabel's use of information shows a dual role that many information professionals have to master: being an acknowledged source of information expertise while at the same time mainstreaming themselves within a larger organisation with broader goals. At the end of the day, the aim is to provide the best advice to clients on legal matters and that cannot be done without accurate, timely and, above all, reliable information. The enquiry cycle means that it is necessary to clarify the query, consult the available sources, use judgement in analysing the information returned and return the output of that work to the client.

Clarify the query

An old adage of the library world is that what people say they want isn't necessarily what they really want. Getting good quality information about the query to begin with will change the way in which it is handled. This means learning about the wider picture that is the full story of the case involved and the particular nuances of this enquiry in relation to that case. This in turn means methodical questioning and working methods, utilising skilled reference interviewing techniques. Fleshing out the query will give an idea of the correct path to follow in researching information to answer it.

Consult the sources

While many of the paper-based sources in law are well established, the increasing use of electronic, Internet-based resources and the need for more research information to provide background to a case place a greater emphasis on keeping up to date:

> We would take it in turns to learn more about a particular database and share it with the rest of the team. That worked well as everyone had to get to grips with something and had a

bit of ownership of it. It became increasingly difficult to keep up with all the databases, so it was useful to have a specialist to ask when you got stuck.

During the period, support for staff dealing with enquiries has changed from a paper-based crib sheet giving a first point of call for various enquiries to dedicated corporate intranet pages with links to key databases, selected Internet resources offering free information such as government publications and advice on search strategies for different services.

Judgement

Assessing quality and authoritativeness of sources is vital to providing accurate answers to queries, information to lawyers and advice to clients. It is necessary to be sure that you have explored as many avenues as possible, as mistakes cannot be tolerated. However, it is important to bear in mind that sometimes there may not be an answer to an enquiry at all: if an issue has not been tested in a court of law, there may not be any information to find. Knowing the sources and how to search them properly reduces any element of doubt, so that when you cannot find any further information, you can be sure that it is because there isn't any more to find.

This is where differences between information professionals and users show up, as the rise of electronic resources has meant that expectations have been raised. For example, access may be provided to electronic abstracting and indexing services of journals and each service will only cover certain journals over a specific time period. An enquiry may lie outside the scope of these sources, which someone using them from their desktop may not appreciate. Similarly, a database may have the text of Acts of Parliament and Statutory Instruments in their original version, whereas an enquirer may need the amended, up-to-date version which is elsewhere, perhaps in another database. This obviously creates a training need: with more and more services being available to people from their desks, users are no longer dependent on a physical resource in a library where an information professional may be on hand to guide them.

Output to client

Having found what you believe to be the most accurate, up-to-date and relevant information, this must be passed on to the enquirer in a suitable form. It is now possible for information to be passed on very quickly via e-mail to a lawyer and then onto a client. This saves much time as well as resources in terms of photocopying, and printing, but can also raise issues such as copyright.

This has also raised expectations, meaning that people expect to be able to get answers to their queries from the best sources instantly. All of this is in the context of a commercial environment, where you know that if your firm is not able to provide a fast and efficient service, one of your competitors will. As Annabel says:

> If you are about to leave late in the evening and you get an urgent phone call from a fee-earner working abroad, you would not walk out at that point, you would make sure you got the information for them somehow or other ... our aim was to make sure they had the information they wanted, when they needed it.

This enquiry cycle relies upon clinical dissection of the research problem, an expert knowledge of the available sources, intuition and an ability to think round the query, to judge the information available and to deliver the right answer at the right time in the right format. What is also clear from the experience of Annabel is that the boundaries between information and its users are becoming increasingly blurred: with fee-earners having access to information resources from their desktop, this changes the dynamic of the whole process making it more interactive and challenging traditional roles.

Information services

The rise of web-based resources may be seen by some as a threat to the role of information professionals in the legal profession. However, knowing the sources and how to interrogate them, assessing the quality of the information returned and asking the right questions are just as important in the electronic world as when everything was only available in a physical library.

Corporate intranets mean that pages of links to key resources, usually databases, are available throughout a firm. This changes the role of the information professional from one of an intermediary into a trainer. However, the proliferation of electronic services means that it is more and more difficult to keep abreast of new developments, even for the professionals.

Portals and one-stop search sites have been mooted as a possible solution to some of these problems, but there are real issues about their prospective use. Users have an imaginary front end in their minds where a single search box using natural language and free text will provide them with exactly what they want by cross-searching all the relevant sources. Many of the electronic sources currently used are very good which has raised expectations, but a computer can only index what is present on a page, in a record or in a database – that is to say the words that are there, not the crucial concepts that may lie behind those words; equally it can return lots of irrelevant information just because a certain phrase is present. Until the cross-searching services can start finding meanings and semantics rather than just text, it means that a role for a highly trained, well-resourced and competent information professional remains.

Future needs

There seems to be a central paradox for the future role of the information professional in the legal field: as more information resources become available in electronic form accessible from people's desktops, the need for their skills may be seen as decreasing. Yet the reluctance of the average user to learn new information-seeking skills for each new source of information means having someone on hand who can either help the user interrogate the sources in an expert fashion or do it themselves, filtering out irrelevant details and handing the user the information they want, when they want it. This seems to indicate the continuing importance of an intermediary between information and its users. Or as Annabel put it:

> The challenge for information professionals is to keep proving their worth, by acting as filters of information. The difficulty lies in persuading people of your value as they only realise that when they attempt to do it themselves and make a potentially costly mistake ... The job is very different now, as you can get through much more work and get 'an' answer instantly, so you have to adapt your skills to the new arena, especially in the commercial world, as they will always want what their competitors have got, so you've got to provide it for them.

10

Educational usage of economics and management resources in France

Angela Joyce

Note: The views expressed are those of the individuals concerned and not necessarily of the employing organisations.

Background

What happens when most of the Internet is in a foreign language? According to *Global Reach*, the Anglophone world comprised a mere 35.2 per cent of the Internet population in June 2003 and this figure is falling. However, the vast majority of websites are in English. Clearly, most people using websites are probably doing so in a second or third language. This case study is concerned with Francophone users (3.3 per cent of the Internet population) and, in particular, French users of economics and management resources within higher education.

This case study is divided into two parts, the first considering a user of information, the second an information provider. Both people know each other and use similar resources. The content of the sites referenced here is generally in French only, an interesting fact in itself, although more French sites are now offering an English version.

The information user

Mme Prouvoyeur works at an 'Institut Universitaire de Technologie' (IUT), or university institute of technology, which has no exact equivalent in the UK. It offers vocational degrees, normally lasting two to three years. Lecturers carry out teaching but do little research. Most students are 18 to 21 year olds. Classes take up 25 to 30 hours per week, leaving students little time to carry out independent research in the library. Most courses include a placement in industry. Subjects studied include management, computer science, social work and statistics.

Mme Prouvoyeur is the manager of the IUT library; her professional interest lies more in teaching than in library science. She has worked there since 1974 and feels she has grown and developed professionally along with the library. She originally studied geography and has travelled widely, learning English while abroad. She has had some formal library training (CAFB professional certificate in 1977 and a DESS in applied telematics in 1988). Her specialist library subject is management. Her library has only four staff serving the university, which has 1,800 students and 148 permanent academic staff.

Mme Prouvoyeur's job consists of liaising with teaching staff and designing and delivering information skills training to students both within the IUT and beyond. Teaching takes place in the classrooms and is integrated into courses. So, how do French students use information? An average group of students would prefer sites that are fast and simple to use. However, they are gradually showing more interest in gateways, directories and official or academic sites if they can find useful quality information for their courses there. They all use Google in its simple format, rarely in advanced search mode, and are usually in a hurry. Clearly, Mme Prouvoyeur has a challenge: how does she approach this? She tries to encourage her students to break down their assignments into steps: analyse the subject; organise a plan of action; consider the merits of online or paper-based resources; choose which sort of online tools to look at: CDs, Internet, e-mail. She does direct them to the *RIME* gateway (see below) and they are gradually learning to appreciate it. They like to learn about the

Internet, but typical IUT students who do not have the Internet at home still prefer paper journals. She is aware of a rapid growth in the usage of Internet resources, as full-text documents come online, for example, from *INSEE* (the national French statistical service).

Teaching staff have been very reticent about using the Internet for teaching; some do integrate sites into their bibliographies for law and marketing.

As well as teaching information skills to students, Mme Prouvoyeur also liaises with lecturers, organises *XML* courses for librarians and information scientists, is in a library network which works for the *INSEE* site, and contributes resources to the *RIME* gateway. She uses online resources confidently, naming Eudora e-mail, *Google*, *Yahoo* France and the *AlltheWeb* search engine as favourites. She is an avid sharer of bookmarks.

The question of language is interesting. Mme Prouvoyeur believes that there is a long-standing anti-English language feeling in France, despite the popular impression that many people are now keen to speak English (or American). Most of her students will see a site in English and not bother to continue. It is important to know this in advising them in information skills. If this seems narrow-minded, we might remember that many native English-speakers are similarly reluctant to look at a foreign language site.

The information provider

Mme Léon is the manager of an economics and management gateway called *RIME*. RIME is a free quality-controlled gateway of economics and management websites, mainly serving the French higher education community. It has some similarities with the UK social science gateway *SOSIG*, although it is smaller. It does not have any competitors as such. Mme Léon is a qualified university librarian who now works for URFIST (Unité Régionale de Formation à l'Information Scientifique et Technique), an organisation funded by the French Ministry of Education, which educates students, librarians and lecturers in the use of online materials. URFIST also makes available articles by researchers on information skills teaching, digital libraries and resource discovery. There are URFIST regional offices around France.

Mme Léon's work involves organising and teaching information skills courses, resource discovery for economics and law materials, and co-directing various educational Internet gateways. Her academic background is in philosophy and she also completed the *ENSSIB* qualification for university librarians. ENSSIB is one of the French 'Grandes Ecoles' or elite universities. She maintains a strong interest in online educational developments, both in France and outside.

She is happy using many types of online application and spends 80 per cent of her time online looking at educational or academic sites, sometimes using Microsoft Office applications, Google and *Wanadoo* search engines and Eudora e-mail. She has great experience in using subscription databases serving academic libraries. Another resource she uses in her resource discovery work is online reviews of journals. The *University of Tarbes Journal Reviews* provides one such site which offers qualitative reviews of key social science journals from many countries. Other favourite sites are *Le Monde* and *Courrier International*, a French language site that provides summaries of news articles from international sources, in French. She is able to read English too, an advantage in her work, given the number of English sites. Internet bookmarks are important resources for Mme Léon, as they are for Mme Prouvoyeur. Mme Léon uses both her own and those of university librarians, which can often be accessed publicly. She makes hers available on the *URFIST* website. In general, online sharing of bookmarks seems to be a growth area in France.

In terms of professional awareness, she belongs to *ADBS*, the main French association for librarians and information workers. In addition she reads journals such as the ADBS's *Sciences de l'Information*. There are fewer information journals for higher education librarians in France than the UK. Mme Léon attends an event similar to the UK's *Online Information*, called 'I-expo', run by *Groupement Français de l'Industrie de l'Information*.

RIME was inspired by the American Bill Goffe's site, *Resources for Economists on the Internet*. It was started in 1996, to provide a directory of key sites, mainly in French, for economics and management. Sites are reviewed and added by a dispersed team of subject specialists, librarians and lecturers. French sites are a priority, but nearly two-thirds are in English. The gateway is still in its early days in terms of size, with about 700 sites listed. Editors use their own selection criteria and links are checked regularly. Statistics are kept for usage and average page hits per month for 2002 was 4,630. No major user surveys have been conducted yet, although Mme Léon is planning some evaluative activities.

The service is publicised by the parent organisation URFIST, which runs workshops around France at universities or in the Paris office, where there is a training suite. Occasional articles are published in information journals.

In terms of typical usage, RIME is actively promoted only among students of the Troisième Cycle (Third Cycle) and above, roughly equivalent to a doctorate in the UK. Either they are given training by their own librarians or lecturers, or URFIST runs courses or workshops. Intriguingly, while science and humanities students are keen to learn information skills, economics students seem less keen. Mme Léon is not sure why this might be: do economists consider that they can learn these skills independently, as they are trained to handle data and are generally good at analytical thinking? But surely the same could be said of scientists?

The future looks good for RIME, with definite funding, some expansion in the number of sites and the possibility of attracting a larger audience. One plan is to develop a bilingual interface, offering English as well as French descriptions of the sites. But the main aim is still to serve the French-speaking user community.

To conclude, France is embracing the Internet and all it offers as part of wider social and technical changes. There are great efforts underway to organise Internet resources and promote them for higher education, but some traditional attitudes still persist in terms of user skills teaching. Google reigns supreme among students, but staff are trying to promote more selective online services.

11

Finding and managing information for the international community: Barbara

Lesly Huxley

Note: The views expressed are those of the information consultant and do not necessarily reflect those of the FAO.

Background

The Food and Agriculture Organisation (FAO) of the United Nations was established in 1945 with a mandate to 'raise levels of nutrition and standards of living, to improve agricultural productivity, and to better the condition of rural populations'. The FAO is one of the largest specialised agencies in the UN system with over 3,500 staff (approximately half working at the headquarters in Rome). The FAO has 183 member countries plus one member organisation, the European Community. Information is described as one of its four core activities. *WAICENT* (the World Agricultural Information Centre) aims to provide an entry point to all the information the FAO provides directly or by licence and manages and populates a number of databases.

Barbara is a Canadian who has worked for the last two years as an information management consultant in the *AGRIS*/CARIS and Documentation Group, part of the Library and Documentation Systems Division in the FAO's offices in Rome. She has an undergraduate degree in sociology and a Masters in archival studies. Like many working in international organisations, she has had a fairly mobile career pattern, working in multilingual and multicultural environments. Previous jobs have been in agricultural and forestry research and information centres (for other international organisations) in the Philippines and Indonesia, and involved user education and support ('a general orientation to the Internet'). She describes herself as a library and information professional.

Practice

The Library and Documentation Systems Division is concerned with the development of information systems and related user needs analyses, evaluations and guidelines. 'Users' in this context include other FAO staff in Rome and in branch offices and related organisations around the world. Overall, Barbara's role is focused on finding out what kind of information users are looking for and exploring how the FAO's information resources can be better aligned with these needs. Part of that work, as in previous jobs, involves information discovery: 'I spend a lot of time looking for things for other people, I've seen a lot of systems, tried a lot of things.' She also spends quite a bit of time writing reports and requirements papers for which she also has to do research. One example was an evaluation of InfoFinder, one of the FAO's search tools, which was developed in her group. Until recently, Barbara's work involved dealing with e-mail enquiries submitted via a link on the FAO InfoFinder site. Bravely, this encouraged users to ask for help if they couldn't find what they were looking for and generated around 500 e-mail enquiries over a three-month period. The link has now been replaced by a number of FAQs written by Barbara based on the queries received.

Within the Library and Documentation Systems Division, the FAO has a library that deals with more in-depth subject enquiries. While Barbara's group is responsible for managing the *AGRIS* database and cataloguing (into the library database) recent reports and other FAO documents, the library's holdings include less recent and 'physical' assets such as books and paper reports. The two departments are physically separated but work together wherever appropriate.

Barbara has just completed a user survey project focusing on the information needs and practices of delegates at two recent FAO conferences. Users here were senior staff from member countries, including representatives of branch offices, NGOs (non-governmental organisations) and related centres. The survey involved a paper-based questionnaire and a number of follow-up interviews, the results of which Barbara was happy to share as we talked.

Barbara describes her own use of the Internet and Internet-based information resources as 'very good' compared with the general population but 'something less' than those of a reference librarian. She learnt her Internet skills and became familiar with a range of online services through her work in the Philippines, where she acknowledges the valuable support and encouragement given by her boss. Barbara's skills, knowledge and experience came in very useful in dealing with the e-mail enquiries, and also meant that there were some surprises for her in the results of the user survey. As we'll see, the economic situation of information users and local infrastructure affect Barbara's ability to respond to information requests.

Using information

Information requests and sources

Most of the e-mail user information requests related to very specific topics rather than broad areas requiring in-depth research and subject knowledge. Examples include details of food grade regulations for sodium silicate, non-approved food additions and specific copyright permission queries. The most requested information was factual or statistical, such as: 'How many livestock are there in Zambia?', 'How many oranges does Spain produce?' or 'What is the number of food insecure people in the world, broken down by major regions, in the last decade?' Barbara often uses the *AGRIS* database but it usually takes a lot of work to actually retrieve the resources described in it. Much of the information is available through the FAO website, but as Barbara remarks, 'there are almost half a million pages on the FAO site: it's often not so much people don't know what they're looking for, they just can't find it.' On the other hand, Barbara is very familiar with most of the FAO's information services:

> ...it's easy for me, I know the FAO site very well. I know, for example, that most of the statistics are in FAOStat, but that's hard to find if you don't know where to look. I suppose a third of the time I just know where to go to get the information, and a third I'd need to search.

As well as searching through the FAO's own data sources, Barbara uses publications databases, electronic full-text searches and database searches. She also finds Google very useful when a full-text search is necessary: 'Google works really well for full-text searches.' The remaining third of e-mail enquiries were forwarded to the FAO library: these were from users who knew they wanted information in a broad area but didn't quite know exactly what.

Variation in response

The source of the enquiry impacts on where Barbara searches and the kind of information she is able to pass on. If the request is from a developing country, she might spend a little more time on the search as 'they don't have many options'. By this she means a number of things: they don't necessarily have access to local facilities such as a library (although she may refer them to one of the UN depository libraries), and their financial resources are also extremely limited. This is a problem common to many of those wanting access to FAO information: 'many people requesting information do not have money to pay' for information. 'Sometimes I might find a reference in AGRIS and then try to find it in other sources where you can get it electronically for free.' The economic situation and local infrastructure also affect the kind of information requested: about a quarter of the enquiries were completely outside the FAO's domain, such as details about obscure chemicals or building materials. Even so, Barbara often did brief searches to try to meet their needs if from a developing country, particularly if she just happened to know a site already that would provide the information. The 'few options' open to these users seemed to mean that the invitation to e-mail a query was an opportunity not to be ignored.

Users' information use

On the whole, the users submitting e-mail enquiries were looking for information to support their day-to-day work, such as report writing. In these cases, most also generally wanted a quick answer: 'Sometimes they'll say "it's urgent, it's for a report I'm doing, I need this right now". I find people in developing countries are a bit more patient.' Interaction with users here was fairly straightforward, as she doesn't feel she has the in-depth subject knowledge to provide commentary or analysis, although would let people know if a document she had sent was a draft or soon to be updated.

Those surveyed from the conferences wanted material to support meetings and conference attendance, or simply to keep up to date in their subject field. These are senior staff who often have secretaries or other assistants who point them in the right direction for information from the FAO website. They also 'know a lot of people, so if they don't find what they're looking for, they can call someone and ask'. All the same, three-quarters of this group were using the Internet at least weekly. Barbara was also surprised at their reported (and observed) browsing preferences over searching. She puts this down to their not necessarily knowing what the search box is searching (that is, a database or full-text searching) and browsing allows people to get a feel for what's available without being overwhelmed with too many results. One participant in the recent survey at the FAO said that when he is searching, he doesn't know what term to use (such as GMO or genetically modified organisms). Another said it was difficult for her to find information on communication for development as she also didn't know what terms to use. Another said that he uses a search engine if he doesn't see a link to what he wants.

> Well, I guess searching is ... an advanced skill. People like reference librarians, people who are familiar with a database, they know what they're doing with a search ... Users want to search for something sometimes but don't know what controlled terms are used, they don't know what term to put in, offering browsing choices (through navigation or a Yahoo-like subject tree), means they don't have to guess the terms.

Awareness of the different databases available and what they contain appears to be low (for example, what is available in the Library catalogue, the AGRIS database or departmental databases). All FAO documents should be available in English, French, Spanish, Chinese and Arabic, but the levels of coverage can vary due to the resources necessary to provide information in five languages, particularly for less high-profile items. However, even where full-text documents are not available in all official languages, some databases are indexed with the FAO's *AGROVOC* thesaurus where all subject keywords exist in English, French, Spanish, Arabic and Chinese so that the subject coverage is available in the five official languages. Keywords and classification are important elements of successful information discovery: Barbara has to search across many different sources with different controlled vocabularies, including those where users using local systems are indexing material themselves with their own subject keywords and indexing practices. This makes Barbara's and others' search tasks more complex. Perhaps reflecting browsing preferences but also this search complexity, the users surveyed wanted to see more subject-themed material rather than just a search engine.

Information services

What implications do Barbara's work and needs have for information services? One of the key areas of impact is for user interface design and the need to make services more intuitive to use, incorporating both searching and browsing features. User-centric design is important: the FAO's website, for example, often presents information according to its internal divisions and structures which mean little to those unfamiliar with it.

Barbara is dealing with a range of different users and notes the different needs they have of the same systems and the implications this has for system design and in particular information organisation:

> AGROVOC ... is a corporate tool used in varying degrees throughout the organisation, and both press releases and technical departments are indexed using it. However, in the case of press releases, access to the terms 'beekeeping' or 'peanuts' is more appropriate than 'apiculture' or 'groundnuts' which are appropriate for indexing technical documents. In AGROVOC, apiculture and groundnuts are the preferred terms, and beekeeping and peanuts the second term (non-preferred). But you have to know what to search for, which is the preferred term.

The sheer volume of services and their specialist content suggests, however, that 'dumbing down' interfaces may not always be of most benefit to users. Intermediaries like Barbara and subject librarians still have a place in these specialist areas and can save users time and money with efficient and knowledgeable searches.

The second major lesson learned from Barbara's practice and the needs of her users relates to infrastructure and, again, money. Where information is freely available and connections are fast, users do not really have to want the information too badly to get it. Priorities change where connections are slow and/or information comes at other costs such as subscription or copy fees: users then need to be serious about wanting the information rather than just 'being curious'. She notes that the connections in Indonesia were really slow 'so you had to know what to look for if you didn't want to waste half a day'. This experience is borne out by her current working environment:

> Most African countries do not have good access. An issue often discussed when there is a need for software is whether to develop something ourselves or choose an open source option, or to purchase a commercial product. While sometimes

> developing something internally may have disadvantages, it allows us to allow our member countries to use them, [because] there aren't any copyright issues.

So not only are Barbara and her colleagues providing important information mediation services in terms of subject and search knowledge, they are also providing tools designed specifically for local distributed use in areas where tools and international connections are not yet readily available or robust.

12

From practice to need – some reflections

Lesly Huxley

The case studies in the preceding chapters illustrate some of the diverse uses and users of social science information. For some, there is a need for in-depth, comprehensive searches, analyses and interpretations, while for others short, sharp fact-finding is a dominant activity. Some, of course, have varying needs for combinations of these. In our introduction we promised the reader surprises: the range, perceived value and social and economic contexts of the tasks and sources reported in the preceding chapters certainly give pause for thought. This chapter provides an opportunity to do just that, to reflect on any emergent themes of user practice and need that impact on the development and delivery of social science information services.

As 'digital Darwinism' (a need for the fittest to survive) fosters greater collaboration between services – and interoperability of information becomes more prevalent – the use of information for purposes other than those for which it was originally intended is likely to become more common. Our contention in this book is that an understanding of the range of users' needs and practice will assist information professionals in reassessing their activities. As intended, the case studies provide illustrations, not the basis for generalisation. However, while they reveal some wide variations in need and practice, they do also have some interesting and potentially surprising common themes. Even in our small number of cases, need (in terms of 'doing the job') can be seen to shape practice, as do a range of constraints. The variety of organisational contexts and pressures also has an impact. All report problems of information discovery and selection (where and how to find it, how to know when to stop looking), information management (what to do with it once found or delivered) and various kinds of barriers that impede access to information.

In this chapter I highlight some examples of the needs and practices from the cases that seem to me potentially important for the design and sustainability of social science information services. This is not to ignore the value of the research available on user needs in general, but our focus here is on practice. I wrote much of this chapter just after attending *ECDL2003* and while attending *DigiLib2003*. Both conferences reported the outcomes of studies of user practice from around the world. Many coincided with the notes I had made on our cases: these and other research results are also briefly noted here.

Four themes common to many of the cases struck me in particular and are discussed further in the rest of this chapter:

- the ubiquity and user appreciation of Google in so many different settings;
- the demand for tailored currency and current awareness services (and the concomitant potential for information overload);
- the range and nature of barriers to accessing information; and
- the importance of 'brand', subject knowledge and personal networks to selection, validity and authority judgements.

Simplicity v. complexity; interfaces v. information literacy

It is clear from the cases and from other research that many users find Google eminently usable. While actually a complex animal, Google is appreciated for the simplicity of its basic interface and results sets that 'satisfice'[1] more than other search engines. In an opening keynote at DigiLib2003, Carol Tenopir (Tenopir et al., 2003) notes from her recent research that naive users like Google, even though they may not understand the ranking algorithms that appear to provide relevant results in so many cases. John Lervik (2003), in his ECDL2003 opening keynote, highlighted the importance of delivering deceptively simple interfaces to complex systems for users whose expectations are built on Google. If users believe it will provide 'good' (or 'good enough') results quickly, they are likely to use Google over specialised and more complex sources that may require training in advanced searching to get the best results.

Several of our cases use Google: the FE lecturer does so because he does not need to be 'discriminating'. Authoritative sources for his learning exercises are less important than freely available and interesting topics around which students can develop and practise other skills. Philip Pothen (2003) of the UK *JISC* (Joint Information Systems Committee) noted at DigiLib the work of David Nicholas at London University which reveals an increase in shallow searching: he found that users rarely visit any website in any depth, frequently 'bounce' quickly from one site to another and seldom revisit. The academic in our case study uses Google for 'broad' searches, 'clicking around' and bookmarking sites found for later. Her bookmark collection is becoming increasingly large and unmanageable and she is often unable to find sites again.

With growing universal acclaim, Google may be beginning to acquire the kind of 'brand' validity which, for example, the academic and the journalist in our case studies recognise in key subject sources (people, organisations, publications) that also have a reputable 'offline' brand. From the media consultant we hear that he doesn't visit libraries: his sources are either online or in key printed journals and magazines. The FAO information consultant reports that few of the staff surveyed were aware of the existence of the FAO Library, let alone the numerous specialist databases available to them. The FE lecturer rarely uses the Learning Resource Centre in his college. Students in particular are reported almost always to use Google, to find the results they obtain useful and to need no other source or support.

Yet the news is not all bad for specialist subject services: the FAO information consultant, the media consultant and the EUI research student all confirm the importance of subject-based access to information. Barbara at the FAO comments on the number of users who report a preference for browsing over searching. Her own observations of users interacting with information services confirmed their preference for subject tree navigation. The FAO users surveyed asked for more subject-based access to information. Olaf at the EUI goes further, demanding greater rigour and subject classification and organisation to support independent study. Some users' practice demands a more focused search than can be achieved via Google. An all-inclusive approach is fundamental to the Cochrane group's work, as is the case with the law firm. The FAO users also require specialist information largely held in extensive bibliographic or other subject-based databases (although the information consultant uses the embedded Google toolbar to facilitate searches of the extensive and complex FAO website.

This issue of complexity in service navigation and searching arises in a number of our cases and highlights the importance of usability. The Cochrane Group and the FAO, for example, report the disparate range of service interfaces and complex search mechanisms that they have to address as part of their day-to-day work. Jo, with the Cochrane Library, notes difficulties arising from varying functionality across the number of different sites people need to use and the length of time it takes to learn to use them. Barbara reports similar difficulties with the databases and web interfaces she and her users need to work with. Familiar interface concepts and elements can help users grasp the logic of how services operate. As the media consultant says, if the interface isn't intuitive, 'not right first time', then people are unlikely to use it.

The extent of information literacy training and support that is available (or acceptable) to users also has a part to play here. In some cases we hear from both users and information professionals of a lack of time (or, as the FE lecturer notes, institutional energy) for learning. Others feel less of a need for skills development: Sandeep and Jeremy have strong academic and practice backgrounds and are confident in their information discovery. Barbara, the FAO's information consultant, is largely self-taught and, like Sandra and Wendy, has a nagging feeling that there could be more to learn. Information professionals in areas such as medicine and law express concern that some users (or clients) do not realise that there may not yet be an answer *on the Internet.* Experiences with Google and similar services lead us to expect that there will always be a relevant set of results for any query.

While the Cochrane Group teams work together to share knowledge and skills, Philip Pothen (2003) notes a growing risk to information literacy in education: tutors, for example, are increasingly aware of digital resources, but are passing this information on to students in decreasing numbers. If students continue not to go to the physical library, there is a risk that they (and possibly staff) will become increasingly information poor unless librarians can become more involved in outreach 'out there'. He touched on contexts for information services, including the government push towards lifelong learning and the need for 'joined-upness' of different public services.

So the key messages from this point of reflection are rather contradictory: some users' practices require simple keyword searches and are not too discriminating about the results, while others demand greater precision, comprehensiveness and the ability to access information from a subject perspective. Some users are satisficed by confidence in their own skills and in the results returned by services such as Google, others would welcome more skills development but do not have time to learn. All would prefer some simplification and greater homogeneity of interface. There are implications here too for the 'interface' between users and information professionals which we return to in the final chapter of this book.

Currency and current awareness

Currency and current awareness are both drivers for information seeking and criteria for filtering the resources found. Several of the cases report a need to keep up to date (media consultant, FE lecturer, law manager, trade union researcher and the users of the FAO site, as reported by the FAO information consultant).

Getting the information fast (that is, as soon as it is available) is key in this respect and is achieved in a variety of ways including e-mail alerts and news digest services. Subject-specific services are seen as very important for current awareness. The downside to keeping up to date is the large amount of information that is 'pushed' to users via e-mail and other alerting services. Combined with the results of users' own searches, this is a significant body of information to assimilate, organise and manage.

Users are under considerable time pressure to produce press releases, articles, reports and advisory services and do not necessarily have the time to undertake regular and frequent searches for the latest news across a number of sources. Jeremy challenges information professionals to make life easier for users by providing digests and 'horizon scans', lists of 'hot topics' that synthesise recent trends in a given area. DigiLib presentations from the Social Science Information Gateway (*SOSIG*) in the UK and *AVEL*, the Engineering and Sustainability gateway in Australia, noted user evaluation outcomes that have resulted in their offering 'hot topics' listings and subject-specific news services. The time pressures demanded by user practice are also passed on to those in support roles, as the FAO's information consultant points out: '... library support people are supposed to be able to access everything and to do it yesterday'. Barbara at the FAO and Jeremy, the media consultant, both report that they are often asked questions outside their domain simply because users 'don't think they have time themselves'.

Eason et al. (2003) reported on an evaluation of *Zetoc* use at DigiLib2003. This table of contents alerting service from the British Library has both passive and active users. The evaluation concluded that the passive majority make little use of alerts, while active users often try to follow-up notifications with a request for the full-text item. Information overload and lack of resource (institutional subscriptions, for example) are some of the reported reasons for passive users' lack of follow-up in this way. For information services, there is also the potential impact of raising user expectations by offering such alerting services: even the passive users of Zetoc *want* to be able to find full-text items yet face barriers to doing so.

Our cases indicate a growing need for tailored current awareness services, in part due to a rise in evidence-based policy and practice, in part due to 'traditional' professions where case law or previous research findings are the key to subsequent decision-making. Information professionals need to be behind this current awareness activity, adding value through 'electronic outreach', that is targeted push not pull services. It is important that people use virtual library services appropriately and value them; it is not necessarily so important to bring them within the physical walls of the library or other information repositories. The notion of targeting is an important one here to avoid information overload. Targeted information needs to be balanced with options for spreading the net, to avoid 'undiscovery' – where users may be herded in one direction only to miss other relevant material. The way ahead may be to combine tailored current awareness services with intuitive, subject-based search and browse functionality to support information discovery beyond the user's current expressed profile.

Barriers to information

A lack of time is something most of us complain about and our cases are no exception. They are trying to cope with the deluge of information they are finding for themselves and that is being 'pushed' at them by alerting services the instant new resources become available. I have already talked at length about the barriers put up by complex and very diverse interfaces to content and a disinclination to acquire new information discovery skills. Many of these barriers are also reflected in Eason et al.'s conclusions on better serving Zetoc's passive majority of users, so I make no excuse for including Table 12.1, showing barriers and potential solutions from the concluding slide of their DigiLib2003 presentation. Although the opportunities listed are intended for Zetoc improvements, they are generic enough to apply to any information service.

Table 12.1 Table of barriers and opportunities in addressing Zetoc's passive user majority

Barriers	Opportunities
Local library resources	Make it worth their while
Awareness	Deliver through what they use
Minimum effort to experiment	No major step-functions, e.g. registrations
Minimum effort to manage	Service help to filter, store, etc.
Low tolerance of failure	Cut out early likely failure routes
Linking, inter-system usability	Consistency, common language, etc.

From Eason et al. (2003).

Pressures of time can also be exacerbated by conditions of access to resources online: the information consultant, for example, reports the limited and slow access experienced by herself when working in Indonesia and by her users in Africa and other developing countries. Olaf's propensity to download journal articles and build up his own private archive (with related copyright and licensing issues) is also the result of slow Internet connections that he expects to find when he returns to Poland.

Those who do not have ready access or unlimited time to undertake unskilled searches themselves value information professionals' skills and knowledge. The increasing ubiquity of Internet access may have had a greater impact than we recognise on users taking it for granted. Network access is not as much a given elsewhere as it is increasingly becoming in the UK. There, are, however, still limitations in the UK as we hear from the FE lecturer: the extent to which he can use Internet resources in the classroom is limited by 'institutional inertia' and the availability of personal computers and network access outside dedicated IT rooms. Volunteers in the Cochrane Group are also dependent on resources available to their host organisations: institutional subscriptions to databases and journals online are something of a lottery, a point also raised by the FAO's information consultant about users in developing countries. The latter's access to local resources, such as public libraries, may be limited: their ability to pay for information is restricted and impacts on the kind of information service the FAO and similar organisations can provide. Barriers to information also affect user behaviour and interactions with information services. As we have seen, Olaf is building up a considerable personal archive as insurance against poor Internet access, while Jeremy and Barbara experience queries outside their domain because of users' lack of time or access to information services.

The international case studies here echo many of the common UK themes: one additional issue that users in non-English-speaking countries have to face is the language of the Internet. The French information user and provider both note a desire to provide information services and content in their own language, something that can be difficult when a large proportion of Internet-accessible material in particular is in English. Language may be even more of a barrier for those in the developing world: although the FAO's documents should be available in the UN's official languages, often only the more high-profile documents are fully translated or translated quickly (and who is to say what is high profile?). The use of multilingual thesauri can have a positive impact at least in locating relevant resources, as is shown in the use of *AGROVOC*. Olaf also sometimes has problems with viewing special character sets such as Polish or German because of a need to change browser settings manually. Content and service providers do not necessarily make it easy for non-English speakers to access information.

Validity and authority (or who you know)

In our cases, many people based their information-seeking behaviour on an often implicit form of marketing – personal networks. They know someone who is likely to know someone or somewhere where the relevant information can be found, even if they do not know it themselves. Barbara notes this of senior users of FAO services, and Jeremy, Sandra, Wendy and Olaf report similar approaches. There is recognition, then, of the continuing importance of personal networks in information seeking and judgements about information found. 'Branding' – or perhaps what in other spheres might be called 'provenance' or 'authority' – appears to play a role in judgements of quality and selection, in helping to shape information-seeking and retrieval behaviours. Subject or domain knowledge (in which I include personal networks) is either expressed as a need or as a practised information discovery method. The journalist's selection criteria include known journals or people who have a reputable 'life' offline. Sandeep, the trade union researcher, also uses authority and established reputation as a selection criterion.

Interface issues arise here too: the academic reports that she often cannot find people, as websites aren't always geared up to help visitors find contact details, another reason for Sandra to ask others. Peter mentions that he finds information by 'putting the name in' and following connections from there, from people and their work. Olaf also works in this way. This ability to be able to track back to familiar and trusted sources is seen to be important. While Semantic Web technologies have developed to help make these connections, they have yet to be plugged into mainstream services on a large scale. The low 'brand presence' of libraries, information professionals and information skills to the point that several of our cases report that they don't use (or need to use) them at all is a serious cause for concern, but also an opportunity.

Summary

So far we have offered some examples of user need and practice in the social sciences and considered in broad terms some of the potential implications for service provision and support. For example, usability and accessibility are topics emerging from several of my four themes above. Access to information by subject and the importance of metadata are also revealed to be important aspects of effective current awareness services, managing information overload and the identification of authoritative sources. Another emergent topic is the potential for greater, targeted marketing and awareness-raising both of online services and what they offer alongside Google, and of the value of the advanced search and information management skills information professionals can provide. This is not necessarily to encourage more users to visit the physical library (which may be a lost cause for many users of social science information) but to encourage appreciation and provision of virtual services and their establishment as trusted sources. Implicit throughout is the need for services and activities to be evaluated against real user needs and practice.

The following chapters in Part 2 review in greater depth the topics that we believe are important in the development of information services. Some of these emerge from the case studies while others derive from our own knowledge and experience in delivering information services for social scientists, and our technical and information research and development. At the end of the book, we return to some of the themes noted here and explore how user practice and need, in the changing contexts of society and technology, impact on information services and the role of information professionals.

Note

1. Satisfice: 'To accept a choice or judgment as one that is good enough, one that satisfies. According to Herbert Simon, who coined the term, the tendency to satisfice shows up in many cognitive tasks such as playing games, solving problems, and making financial decisions where people typically do not or cannot search for the optimal solutions.' *Source*: *The Penguin Dictionary of Psychology* (1995).

Part 2
The information issues

The following ten chapters look in more detail at some of the most important issues in running online information services. They have been written by practitioners who have sought to reflect on their own experience and on that of the case studies in order to give the reader clear and relevant summaries of best practice.

13

Effective online information services management

Sue Timmis and Debra Hiom

> Library management culture tends to focus on functions and processes rather than goals and results. (Deegan and Tanner, 2002: 228)

Information professionals have a wealth of expertise in managing library services. However, embarking on online service development involves changes in both mindset and practice. Online information services are a growth area in the fluid Internet environment. This area is characterised by rapid shifts; new products are coming onto the market, new technologies and standards are being developed. You need to be aware of any new opportunities offered by change and be flexible enough to exploit them. In practical terms, this may mean delivering services to new audiences, incorporating new data structures and inter-working with services that may be based on different technologies.

Online information services can range in size and complexity from small-scale projects that an enthusiast embarks upon in their own time to the development of full-blown services at a national level. This chapter is primarily concerned with the development of larger-scale services. However, many of the issues are equally applicable to a project set up by a single person. We will consider how to plan, manage and evaluate your online information service. Given the breadth of this area we will aim to introduce you to all the main issues and provide signposts to further information.

Stakeholders and audiences

Online information services do not exist in isolation or for their own sake. They are always part of a broader context and it is important to define that context and the groups of people who will be involved or affected by the service – that is, your stakeholders. These might include funders, potential users of the service, managers, related support staff and external partners. (The potential of external partners came out particularly strongly in the case studies with Jeremy and Wendy, to add both content and authority to an online resource.) It is essential to document who your stakeholders are and their relationship to the proposed service, as they will need to be involved in different stages and aspects of its development. In particular you will need to identify relevant reporting, decision-making and consultative channels to secure agreement about how it works at the strategic level (something Peter feels may not be fully in place in further education – see Chapter 3).

> **Top Tip**
> Be sure to document your stakeholders and their relationships to the service.

A subset of your stakeholders will be your intended audience and the needs of this audience must inform both the planning and the implementation of your service in order to ensure that it is fit for the purpose. There is a danger of making assumptions about your audience and their expectations (see many of the following chapters for more information). Remember, too, that you may have multiple audiences and that these are likely to be on a global scale. The information you have gathered on your users should then be used to inform all aspects of your service planning.

Aims and objectives

At the outset you will need to define both your aims and your objectives. Aims should encapsulate the overall goals and vision for your service. Objectives are the route by which you achieve your aims and need to cover all aspects of the overall goals. Often these are at risk of being wide-ranging and rather broad statements that require further clarification. A measurable set of scheduled deliverables can help focus the general aims and objectives. Deliverables are an important part of the planning process and are often required as a condition of funding – whether this is from external sources or the allocation of internal resources.

Objectives should be SMART:

- Specific
- Measurable
- Achievable
- Relevant
- Time-based.

Making your objectives SMART can help everyone involved, both in the implementation and in the funding of the project.

It is important to spend adequate time formulating these and consulting with your stakeholders to ensure they represent the shared goals. If you are clear about your aims and objectives at the outset the planning process will be relatively pain free.

Planning

The key tasks and phases of developing an information service might include:

Phase 1: Pre-project:

- Outline planning of project
- Securing funding for project
- Producing outline project timetable and plan

Phase 2: Project planning and set-up:

- Drawing up detailed timetable and plan
- Hiring staff and developing skills

- Developing policy documents
- Technical planning

Phase 3: Technical implementation:

- Technical set-up and system testing
- Training of non-technical staff in system usage

Phase 4: Service development:

- Development and implementation
- Service launch

Phase 5: Day-to-day running:

- Ongoing service development
- Collection management
- Evaluating performance and impact
- Research and development
- Monitoring external drivers

Generally the phases above are all sequential and related, so Phase 3 can't really be started until Phase 2 has been completed, and so on.

Once an overall plan has been drawn up, the next stage is to develop a timetable for development and delivery. There are a few issues to consider here, the most important being that once you have an agreed timetable then you are bound by it. There may be some flexibility in the schedule, but generally deadlines should be kept to in order to avoid development running into timetabling difficulties. There is little point in having lots of important sounding deliverables and a very detailed schedule if this is impossible to meet. It is a guaranteed way to increase the chances of failure. Do not agree to do something unless there are sufficient time and resources available to deliver.

Top Tip
Ensure your plans are realistic rather than ambitious.

Structured project management or methodology tools are available that may help, such as (in decreasing order of formality) *PRINCE2, Dynamic Systems Development Method* and *Extreme Programming.*

Roles and responsibilities

Annabel (see Chapter 9) emphasises the importance of managing staff, workloads and skills in order to deliver a consistently effective resource. Table 13.1 outlines some of the possible roles and skill sets involved in developing and running a service, many of which are covered in more detail in the following chapters.

Ideally you would be able to draw on the specialist skills of all those people outlined in Table 13.1. The real world dictates that more often than not you will be working with a smaller group of multiskilled people. This requires the team to have a very broad range of expertise and experience. It can also mean the development of a tight-knit, well-focused team.

When skills are lacking within the core team, it can often be very effective to bring in experts from outside. These experts could be drawn from within the same organisation or they could be commercial consultants. People involved in the technical implementation, user interface design and publicity and promotion are often brought in under such circumstances.

Running your service

The service's strategic objectives need to be realised in day-to-day decisions. This means that all staff in the service have to be aware of the objectives and how they relate to their own decisions. For example, the choice of hardware needs to be informed by plans for growth, the choice of software must take account of the costs of inter-working with other services and the choice of metadata standards depends on users' search requirements and on the cost limitations for metadata creation.

Table 13.1 **Roles and responsibilities relevant to running an online information service**

Title	Description	Skill set
Project manager	Someone to oversee the whole project and ensure the smooth day-to-day running of the service	Organisational skills, good written and oral communication, person management, subject and technical knowledge and understanding, excellent information management skills
Content or subject specialists	Person or persons to develop the scope of the service	Excellent subject knowledge, understanding of information management issues, ideally some web experience and knowledge
Information workers	Person or persons directly involved in the entry of resources into the catalogue (often the same as the subject specialist)	Subject knowledge, confident web user, some understanding of technological principles behind service
Technical implementation officers	Person or persons involved in the development and implementation of the technical side of the service	Excellent technical understanding of the networked environment, good programming and scripting skills and good working knowledge of proposed technology. If developing new technologies then very high network-related technical skills are essential. Ideally some appreciation of information management issues
Technical support officers	Person responsible for the day-to-day technical integrity of the system	As technical implementation officers but can be slightly less experienced if correct tools are put in place in the system development
Web server administrator	Person responsible for the running and administration of the web server	As above plus excellent web server administration skills
User interface designers	Person or persons responsible for the design and implementation of the user interface	Good understanding of website design and well versed in usability and accessibility issues
Finance officer	Person responsible for the financial side of the project	Good understanding and experience of potentially large-scale project financial management, may or may not be project manager
Marketing officers	Person or persons responsible for the development and deployment of publicity and promotional materials/activities	Experience in publicity and promotions, good subject knowledge and user community understanding

Adapted from DESIRE (2000).

To ensure effective day-to-day running of the service you always need to have an eye on future developments. A learning organisation has been defined as an establishment 'which harnesses the full brainpower, knowledge and experience available to it, in order to evolve continually for the benefit of all its stakeholders' (Mayo and Lank, 1994; see also Chapter 25). This is particularly pertinent for the online information services environment where technology and practices are continually changing. *Investors in People* (IIP) is a UK national standard which sets a level of good practice for the training and development of people to achieve organisational goals. If you are a small team, the IIP standard may be too unwieldy but there are several steps you can take to ensure that you are working within the principles of the IIP. These include:

- induction of new staff;
- initial training and development of new staff in basic knowledge, skills and attitudes to carry out job;
- ongoing training and development to improve current performance or overcome identified weaknesses;
- training and development to cope with expected changes in the organisation's structure, policy, products or services;
- induction and initial training and development to support changes in job role;
- a range of development opportunities (such as job shadowing) open to all.

Ensuring good communication within the team is also a key task for the manager, which may not always be easy to achieve, especially as members of the team may be from a variety of disciplines with their own terminology, assumptions and personalities. Keeping staff informed about the changing context in which they are working, and how their individual contributions affect the overall effectiveness of the service, will encourage people to keep engaged in ongoing development. Of course, your team may well be geographically distributed and keeping them well informed will need extra effort. Perhaps one of the greatest drawbacks of running a distributed team is dealing with the problems of working remotely. The job requires that staff should be self-motivated, yet it is very easy for staff to feel isolated without the advice and support of colleagues around them. A geographically dispersed team will rely heavily on remote communication through one-to-one e-mail contact, telephone and the use of mailing lists and/or web conferencing systems for 'virtual meetings'.

And it is not only the team that may be remote – users can be too. 'The more services that are provided electronically, and the less need to visit a physical place, the less their users may be aware who provides those services' (Deegan and Tanner, 2002). The relative 'invisibility' of online services provides a real challenge and you need to ensure that you maintain a high level of engagement with your users to combat this lack of physical presence. Chapter 15 provides you with some ideas on understanding your markets and effective promotion of your service.

Monitoring and evaluation

An essential requirement for the effective management of any service is a clear sense of purpose and progress, together with an understanding of current strengths and weaknesses and well-defined mechanisms for improvement. As Jeremy implies (see Chapter 6), when running an online service, these requirements become even more important because of the need to be responsive to evolving user needs and the opportunities afforded by the technology itself. There is also a need to keep apace with new standards, legislation and policies, which in their turn are also subject to frequent changes as technology develops and impacts on our working practices.

Evaluating the work you do and the service you develop is an essential part of the management brief. Developing an evaluation plan will ensure that you are monitoring and assessing your service in both a planned and comprehensive way. Systematic evaluation of your service will also allow you to identify where and how improvements should be made. In addition, whoever has provided the budget or funding to run this service will want to be kept informed of progress and is likely to impose a reporting and monitoring structure for this purpose.

> **Top Tip**
> Systematic evaluation is essential to keep your service up with expectations and regulations.

So what is evaluation, and how do you go about developing an evaluation plan? There is a lot of mystique about this topic and it is often seen as something very rarefied and difficult to understand. In truth, evaluation is very straightforward: it is about examining, exploring and understanding how your project is working.

However, it is also about making judgements on its effectiveness, allowing you to use this information to make improvements and amendments where needed. Chambers Dictionary's definition of evaluation is 'to determine or estimate the value of'. This value judgement is a crucial aspect of evaluation that must be understood and incorporated into your activities. In other words, it is not sufficient to examine and explore your project in some detail, you must also reflect on what this tells you and identify an appropriate response.

Evaluation planning

The best way to approach this is to develop an evaluation plan which will amplify the why, who, how, what, when questions and ensure that your evaluation activities are linked together and connect to the aims and objectives of the service. An evaluation plan usually contains the following sections:

1. *Statement of aims and objectives for service*
   - This is an important starting point because you need to be clear about how your evaluation activities will support your overall aims and objectives.

2. *Overall aims and objectives for evaluation*
   - In this section, you will identify what you want to achieve by undertaking the evaluation. This can often be closely linked to section 3.
3. *Key evaluation questions*
   - It is important to clarify precisely what questions you are attempting to answer through your evaluation – see Table 13.2 for some examples of questions you might ask. These can be divided into internal questions, where you are evaluating your own efficiency and effectiveness, and external questions, where you are evaluating the impact that your service has on users and stakeholder groups.
4. *Identified methods*
   - A range of methods is usually employed depending on the nature of the evaluation questions you are addressing. Some typical examples might be analysing web statistics, gathering and analysing performance indicators, analysing help desk queries, undertaking a survey of stakeholder views, holding a focus group to elicit user views.
5. *Time-based evaluation plans (typically annual)*
   - These plans need to spell out exactly how each evaluation question will be addressed. Plans will usually cover the following areas: evaluation focus (or question), success criteria, evaluation instruments, internal reporting procedures (what and to whom), external reporting procedures (what and to whom), timing, resource requirements. In some cases, it may also be useful to identify risk factors. However, first and foremost, the plan needs to be useful and meaningful for you as the manager and your team, and should clearly set out what needs to be done, how and when.

Table 13.2 Typical evaluation questions

Internal evaluation questions
■ Are our activities enabling us to achieve our objectives?
■ How do we determine success?
■ In which areas do we need information?
■ How does our performance compare to previous performance?
■ How can we improve efficiency?
■ How robust are our technical systems?
External evaluation questions
■ Are we reaching our identified target audiences?
■ Is our user base increasing over time?
■ How satisfied are our users?
■ What areas would they like to see improved?
■ How effective are our communications with funders and other stakeholders?

Approaches to evaluation and monitoring

The choice of methods and approaches may be influenced by many issues, such as time available, existing activities that can be repurposed or reused for data gathering, the expertise available and the budget you have for evaluations. For example, it is no use planning a large-scale survey of national and international users of your service if you have no budget, time or resources available to support this major undertaking.

It is, however, also important to choose methods that will enable you to gather meaningful and useful data. Performance indicators are often cited as 'obvious' approaches to evaluating information services. For example, Chowdhury and Chowdhury (2003) have said that digital libraries should be judged on their success in retrieving relevant results and by the associated time, effort and costs. Furthermore, performance indicators are likely to be requested for monitoring purposes by funders, senior managers and/or budget holders. However, these can be misleading and require lengthy interpretation. Perrin (2002) states that in evaluating innovations, there is a tendency to focus only on success and conclusions are often based on mean (or average) scores where only 'good' scores are valuable. Perrin argues that innovation by its very nature is risky and likely to fail, so that we should focus on how much attempt has been made to learn from failures (as well as successes), whether future implications have been identified and how much has been learned through the process. For this reason, a mixed methods approach will usually be most suitable, where both quantitative and qualitative methods are employed to provide a holistic picture of your service.

In summary, evaluation is a natural part of the management of online services as it supports the reflection, self-assessment and improvement needed to ensure you learn from and build on both the successes and failures your service comes up against.

Where do I go from here?

Hudson (1999) offers further information on stakeholders and managing external relationships. Friedlein (2001) is a useful guide for project managers setting up a web-based service. Lipnack and Stamps (2000) and Cantu (1997) are useful resources if you are interested in how to develop and manage geographically dispersed teams. The *UK Evaluation Society* website offers further information on evaluation techniques and good practice. The site contains information about the society, membership details and details of the annual conference and other events. There is also a list of other websites and mailing lists related to evaluation.

The following two chapters each focus on a specific aspect of management relating to online information services, selection (or 'collection management') and marketing. There are obviously other aspects to management that have been touched on in this chapter (staff management, for example), but we have judged that they are sufficiently generic for the reader to be referred to a general source such as Jordan and Lloyd (2002).

14

Selection

Neil Jacobs

Any resource needs to have a selection policy or a collection management policy (Jenkins and Morley, 1999). This applies whether the resource has a 'collection' in the traditional sense of that word or not. The selection policy emerges from a consideration of three imperatives:

- the intended audience for the resource;
- the information needs of that audience;
- the aims and objectives of the resource.

Before moving on to the details of a selection policy, any resource manager needs to know explicit answers to these imperatives. The golden rule is, if you can't write each of the answers to these questions on a Post-it, then the answers are not yet clear enough!

Defining the audience

More often than not, a resource will have its audience defined for it, because it will have been set up by a budget holder to fulfil the needs of a specified group. However, the budget holder may well not have defined closely who that group is, how it is composed, what tasks the resource will be called on to support, and so on. This may be a matter for some research or, more likely, something to be sensitive to when conducting outreach activities. However, defining the audience and its needs is an aspect of marketing (see Chapter 15), and a resource manager will need to attend to it in those terms.

Defining the information needs

A target audience will have relatively homogenous information needs, but a resource may have several target audiences. Again, this is a market research issue (see Chapter 15). The key question an information professional needs to ask is: 'How comprehensive does the collection need to be?' Those for the Cochrane and law case studies would need to be fairly comprehensive; others may be working on a more 'satisficing' model, where time is more important than being exhaustive. However, quite often, information users will look to information resources not only to satisfy a number of demands, but also to more subtly define a field for them. For example, Jeremy looks to *The Economist* and the *FT* as boundaries to what he needs to know about. Similarly, Wendy relies on the editorial judgement of national voluntary sector organisations to avoid potential information overload. In many ways, both Sandra and Barbara would like to have such mechanisms for knowing when they have searched 'enough'. In this sense, we should not shy away from the fact that any information resource has a selection policy and is in that sense committed to a particular definition of what is relevant and quality material. Which brings us on to...

Specifying the aims and objectives

Any service starts with aims and objectives, discussed further in Chapter 13. These will emerge from a critical synthesis of:

- the demands of the budget holder/commissioner;
- the needs of defined target audiences;
- professional judgement;
- the requirements of a coherent service; and
- available resources.

Of these, coherence is perhaps the most underrated consideration. Any successful product needs to be seen as having integrity, that is as being a coherent fusion of elements that resonates with people's experience of the real world. Given a large enough marketing budget, of course, people can be persuaded to see coherence where originally they did not, but this is unlikely to be the lot of an online information resource. Instead, the manager needs to try to discover some 'sense' behind the demands of the various stakeholders and create a resource that exemplifies this sense and so has a clear identity of its own, in the way that *The Economist* does for Jeremy (see Chapter 6).

> **Top Tip**
> Try to discover what would bring coherence and a clear identity to your service.

Scope policy

From the aims and objectives, it should be possible to draw up a scope policy. This describes criteria to be used in assessing inclusion and summarises some of the ways in which those criteria might be applied. Table 14.1 gives a list of some criteria, together with examples of questions that might implement them. They can be grouped into issues of coverage (range, content and so on), access (cost, technology and so on), metadata (granularity and so on) and geography. Any real service is likely to have to change, substitute, delete and append to this list.

Selection protocol

Once you have a scope policy in place, the next step is to establish a selection protocol, that is an explicit decision procedure for deciding which resources get included and which do not. An example might be to ask this sequence of questions:

1. Is it in scope?
2. Does it duplicate another resource?

Table 14.1 Criteria for a scope policy

Coverage	
Subject matter	What subject matter is appropriate for the target audiences? Are there any subjects which will be censored (for example, for ethical reasons, such as resources produced by hate groups or resources about bomb-making/paedophilia, and so on)? How important is the subject matter of linked sites?
Acceptable types of resource	What types of resource are appropriate for the target audiences? Is the information scholarly or professional rather than popular? Does the resource contain more than just a list of links? Is the site either proven to be or expected to be durable? Would a resource intended for use by an individual or local group be acceptable? Is it innovative – does it contain breakthrough design elements?
Acceptable sources	Which sources of information are acceptable/appropriate for the target audiences? Are academic, government, commercial, trade/industry, non-profit private sources all acceptable? Are pages maintained by individual enthusiasts (e.g. students) acceptable? Is biased information acceptable, and are opinions and ideologies acceptable?
Acceptable levels of difficulty	What level of resource is appropriate for the target audiences? (For example, users may be schoolchildren, graduates, academics or experienced professionals.)
Advertising	Are resources that contain advertising acceptable? Is there a limit to the amount of advertising that is acceptable? Are there any forms of advertising that will be censored?
Access (see Chapters 16 and 17)	
Cost	How is charging going to affect selection – is the service only going to point to resources that are free to access? Are there any price limits in terms of the access charge? What if resources are under copyright?

Technology	What technologies are appropriate for the target audiences (forms, client-side image maps, databases, common gateway interface (CGI) scripts, Java applications, frames and so on)? What connectivity does your audience have and how will this affect selection? What software do your users have and how will this affect selection? (For example, will resources that work well in graphical browsers but not in line browsers be accepted?) What hardware do your users have and how will this affect selection?
Registration	Will the service accept resources where user-registration is necessary before the resource can be accessed? Is online registration acceptable? If users must negotiate written contracts before access is possible, is this acceptable?
Special needs	Do your users have any special needs that will affect the resources selected (for example, large print or audio options for disabled users)?
Metadata and cataloguing issues (see Chapter 21)	
Granularity	At what level will resources be selected/catalogued? Will resources be considered at the website/usenet group level or the web page/usenet article level?
Resource description	What is the minimum amount of information needed to create a resource description in your catalogue, that is what basic information *must* a resource contain to be selected? (For example, in a WWW document, contact details, last update details.) Is there sufficient information to create a descriptive record? Will the service accept resources with/without specific metadata?
Geographical issues	
Geographical restraints	Are any geographical restraints appropriate for the audiences? Will the service cover information produced locally, from particular countries, particular continents or worldwide?
Language	In which languages are resources acceptable/appropriate to the target audience?

Adapted from DESIRE (2000).

3. Is the content relevant, appropriate, high quality, and so on?
4. Is the content in the right form, for example can results be e-mailed, or is there a current awareness news service?
5. Can it be cross-searched using local portal technology, or can it be embedded in some other way (see Chapter 22)?
6. Is it well supported and likely to remain stable?
7. Is it likely to be around in five years' time?

Similarly, it is likely that collection management procedures will require a deselection protocol, for example if a resource becomes less reliable or disappears altogether! Many valuable resources in the social sciences are run on a shoestring, often in the not-for-profit sector, and their comprehensiveness and even existence can be uncertain over time.

Reassessment: anticipating demand

Little of the above will come as much of a surprise to those running online information services. However, to what extent does it chime with the case studies described earlier? Several of the cases (for example, Sandra and Sandeep) said that the range of information that they needed varied drastically, depending on which of a diverse set of tasks they were focusing on at the time. This is the other side of the coin to the need for coherence discussed above, and this is the tension faced by many service managers in the real world. Their service needs to be coherent, have a clear identity and support users who have fragmented and rapidly changing information needs. A selection policy in these circumstances cannot be limited to static criteria, but must contribute to the goal of the service in a deeper sense. This means not only 'deep branding' (emphasising both value and marketing: see Braunstein and Levine, 2000, and Chapter 15), but also helping users build knowledge over time as they move from project to project. To do this, you will need to anticipate future requirements that are, by their nature, fairly unpredictable. There are two ways of addressing this problem which extend the approaches described above. The first is to be more clever about monitoring current usage (on the basis that the best predictor of future needs is past use), and the second is to get more involved in (that is, provide) the community tools that your users exploit. In a sense, this is where selection, marketing (Chapter 15) and usability (Chapter 16) overlap, because all are at least partly concerned with anticipating demand and providing for it.

So far as monitoring current use is concerned, there is a variety of ways of doing this, with a range of sophistication and a corresponding range of prices. At the most basic level, you can locate the web or database log files for your service (or obtain relevant files from the remote resources accessed by your users), and analyse them yourself using standard office packages such as Excel. Although clumsy and basic, this method should not be underestimated for small services on tight budgets. At the next level, you can use commercial log analysis software, such as *Crystal Reports* or *WebTrends*. Finally, there are extremely sophisticated data mining and clustering packages available which will detect hidden patterns in any dataset (such as log files) and present them clearly to you so that you can track aggregate usage patterns.

Monitoring and surveillance are unlikely to be sufficient, however. The second approach to learning what your users are likely to want is getting more deeply involved in their community – staying one step ahead of your users, knowing what they would find useful before they realise they need it. To do this, there is no real alternative to staying close to users, conducting regular outreach and skills sessions (see Chapter 19), as well as less formal contacts. In terms of technologies, again there is a range of options, from the most basic (and cheapest) to the more elaborate. The most basic, ground-level option might be, as used by Mmes Prouvoyeur and Léon (see Chapter 10), to support bookmark sharing. Again, software is available to support this. Perhaps the best route is to use the Semantic Web *RSS* standard, since this allows bookmarks to be syndicated automatically, but lower tech options are available, for example merely hosting bookmarks as HTML (hypertext mark-up language) files or using sites such as *iKeepBookmarks*. More effective, perhaps, might be to host online community services such as discussion forums, ask-an-expert, tips and advice bulletins, topical 'in-the-news' services, and so on. How does your users' community work? How can you be involved to the benefit of both your users and your service? There are some excellent community resources out there to learn from, for example *AccountingWeb* and *FashionCapital*. There are some useful guides to help you get started, for example Ronan (2003).

> **Top Tip**
> Investigate how your users work as a community to learn what to include in the service.

In Chapter 25, we consider the term 'barefoot librarian' as one way to describe the profession after disintermediation (that is, after the triumph of the end-user), and this term nicely encapsulates a shift to a less separate existence for the profession. For some, it will only be by being an active member of the teams he or she is supporting (both offline and online) that the information professional will know which resources are appropriate to include in their support.

Further reading

Cooke, A. (2001) *A Guide to Finding Quality Information on the Internet: Selection and Evaluation Strategies*, 2nd edn. London: Library Association.

Grimshaw, J. (2000) *How to Find Information – Social Sciences*. London: British Library.

Jacobs, N. and Huxley, L. (2002) 'From static content to dynamic communities: the evolution of networked educational resources', *Online Information Review*, 26 (1): 19–29.

15

Marketing your service

Paul Ayres and Neil Jacobs

This chapter is split into two sections. The first looks at marketing as a management process related to those discussed in Chapter 13. The second describes some marketing activities that are specific to the online world.

Marketing as a management process

The Chartered Institute of Marketing defines marketing as 'a management process which identifies, anticipates and satisfies customer requirements profitably' (Bedwell, 2001). 'Profitably' may be replaced by some other criterion where it is not relevant, such as 'efficiently' or 'giving good value for money'. Looking at this definition, it seems clear that marketing should be right at the heart of an information service. By this, we do not necessarily mean that you should be thinking about designing leaflets as you are planning your selection policy. What we do mean is that thinking about your users, and their individual and collective needs, starts when the service is conceived and does not stop! Since we are focusing on online services, there are particular techniques for doing this, but it is probably worth considering the basics of marketing more generally before looking at those techniques to put them into some kind of context.

Core Knowledge
Marketing is a management process, not an afterthought.

There are a number of elements that go into a marketing plan. Broadly, these are:

1. Identification of the audience
2. Definition of the service
3. Marketing objectives
4. Strategy and tactics
5. Resource implications
6. Evaluation plan
7. Schedule

The first marketing decision you need to make is defining your audience. While for some this may be obvious (it may be written into your contract, for example), for others it may not be. Either way, you will need to look at this audience as being made up of a number of distinct groups that you can identify as having particular needs and who will use your service for particular purposes. Of course, this is where market research might come in but, realistically, that may not be an option. Once you have identified your target audiences, you will need to go through them one by one. Ask yourself the following questions about each:

- What do these people do for which they need information?
- What things have these people got in common?
- How do these things relate to the service I'm offering?
- What would be most valuable to them in an online information service?
- How do they fulfil these needs at the moment?
- How do these people communicate with each other?

Having considered your target audiences, your next step should be to consider your service and where it stands at the moment. There are various well-known techniques for doing this, such as SWOT analysis (Strengths, Weaknesses, Opportunities, Threats) and STEP analysis (Social, Technical, Environmental and Political factors). You should now be able to position the service you're offering in terms of its audiences, its competitors and its 'unique selling point', that is why people would use it rather than any alternatives they may have.

To guide your marketing strategy, you will need to set objectives. The usual acronym used to guide marketing objectives is the same as that used to guide any management objective (see Chapter 12) – 'SMART': Specific, Measurable, Accurate, Realistic, Timely. For example, you might want to increase the use of particular aspects of the service by a specific target audience by a certain amount by a certain date. You can then use the information gathered so far, on the target audiences and the services offered, to develop a strategy to meet those objectives. This may include the online marketing approaches discussed below, and may also include offline marketing using:

- leaflets, for example inserted into delegate packs at meetings and conferences attended by target audiences or publications read by them;
- personal attendance, for example at conferences or by giving training and awareness talks in departments where your target audiences work;
- participating in the life of your target audiences, for example by contributing articles to their journals or newsletters;
- producing your own newsletter for existing and potential users, making sure that its contents are genuinely interesting to them.

Most of these options have resource implications. Successful planning means judging how much resource to devote to each strand in your strategy and having mechanisms in place to monitor the success, and therefore value, that each strand is achieving. Some costs, such as printing leaflets, are obvious. Others are less obvious, such as staff time where people have several roles and do not clearly demarcate dedicated 'marketing time'. Nevertheless, you should at least try to plan the resources for each element of your strategy.

Evaluating your marketing is not the same as evaluating the service (see Chapter 12) and both are important. Since the objectives you set were specific and measurable, it should be possible to say in advance what performance indicators will be used to assess success. However, it is often useful to go behind the figures, to discover why one approach succeeded where another did not. Some insight can be gained by being engaged with your audiences, being in a position to listen to their views without having to make specific efforts. Further information can flow from a well-designed marketing evaluation study, which can form a part of the overall service evaluation (again, see Chapter 12).

Online marketing

So much for the generalities of marketing. There are specific aspects to marketing an online information service or, better, marketing an information service online. These can be divided into those that affect the building of your site, those that aim to attract people to it, those that aim to keep people using it, and those that are concerned with monitoring your marketing.

Building your site

You need to design your website in the correct manner if you are going to market it successfully. One of the first things to do is to choose a name: you need a short and memorable name for your service which translates into a web address that people will find easy to remember and you will find easy to promote.

Another important aspect of building the site is contained in the blue bar at the top of your Internet browser which contains the information in the `<title>` tag of the web page you are looking at, so make the effort to ensure it reflects who you are. Start it with the name of your website or service and then include a short phrase that sums up what you do and what information you provide.

Other HTML metadata tags give you the chance to provide some keywords and a brief description of your site or service. This information is not seen by someone looking at your web page but can be picked by Internet search engines. The most important metadata tags to use are the subject tag, which gives a listing of keywords relevant to your website or service, and the description tag, which includes a short paragraph about your site or service. Chapter 21 gives a more extensive discussion of metadata.

After optimising the HTML tags on your site, ensure that your front page includes some text about who you are and what you do which can be easily picked up by search engines. This is particularly important for database-driven sites, as your carefully crafted content will be hidden behind a search box or dynamically generated web pages. Include some browsable free content that shows off your service which is linked to or featured on your front page.

While usability and accessibility are covered in detail elsewhere, remember that great marketing does not matter if it is difficult for users to do whatever it is you have promised them they can do. They won't come back.

Top Tip

Ensure you have enough text at the top level for peple and computers to recognise your service.

Promoting your service

Once you have built your site, you then have to encourage people to start using it. People need to know about your website, so you need to start getting out in the virtual world and telling other websites and resources about it, a process otherwise known as site submission. A good resource for learning about this is *Selfpromotion.com*, which you can use for 30 days as a free trial, or for ever on payment of a small fee. Other services and guides are also available, perhaps the most well-known guide being from *Search Engine Watch*.

If your service is freely available online, Internet search engines are vital in driving traffic to your site, so make sure you submit your website to them. Do not expect your website to be featured by them straightaway, as it takes some weeks for them to assess your site. The most important search engine is *Google*, but do not neglect others such as *Ask* and *AltaVista*.

Directories are different from search engines (even though they may run search engines over their content), as they are categorised trees of selected websites. The two most important directories to be on are the Open Directory (Netscape's *DMOZ* Project) and *Yahoo*. Here, you will be waiting for real people to assess your site, so it is worth looking very carefully at the selection criteria these sites use. If subject-specific directories relevant to your service exist (for example, via trade or professional associations), make sure you are included on them.

E-mail is a good promotional tool for your service, so include your website address in your e-mail signature and contribute to relevant discussion groups, bulletin boards and other online forums in your subject area. It is a good idea to get other sites to link to your service, so e-mail the webmasters of sites that are similar or related to what you do and ask for a link to your site (for one thing, search engines such as Google rank sites partly according to the number of links to them). This will usually mean that you will have to reciprocate by providing a link to their site, so set up a page of sites you recommend to be able to do this. A good way of doing this is to look at other websites in the directory category you have been included in by *Yahoo* or *DMOZ*.

Providing sticky content

Getting people to your site is one thing, getting them to stay there and to keep coming back is quite another. Content is king and your site or service must have good content to keep people coming back for more. This means that it should be written in a manner that is easy to scan, is browsable by subject, category or type of information, is updated regularly and is appropriate for your intended audience.

You should give people the chance to pass on their e-mail address to receive more information about your site or service or, if you have an existing contacts database, send them a one-time e-mail asking if they would like to know more (though see Chapter 18 concerning the legal aspects of this). You can use the resulting e-mail list in a number of ways. For example, e-mail newsletters can keep people informed about what is going on with your site or service. These might be combined with e-mail alerts updating people about the latest additions to the site. These can be automatically generated by your systems rather than needing to be written by you. Users should be able to pass on their e-mail details and say that, 'I want to receive an e-mail about all new articles in this subsection of your website, every week or month'. These e-mails should contain links back to the relevant parts of your site or service, getting people straight to the content they want. They should be available as plain text as well as HTML, as you cannot guarantee what sort of e-mail package users will be using to view your message.

You should not be afraid to give away content for free. Have copies of your logo that people can download and use as links to your website. If you have a searchable database on your site, make a search box available that people can put on their own websites. Provide standard texts that people can copy and paste so they can refer to your service in a way in which you would approve.

Monitoring and evaluating your marketing

There is little point in expending a lot of time and effort in marketing your website, if you do not evaluate how well you are doing. Check out how many sites are linking to you and hopefully see the number increase over time by running a check at *Linkpopularity.com* or by searching on *Google* using the query:

`<link:www.yourwebsitehere.com>`

However, don't be too dismayed if the figures vary from month to month, as Google changes the way it works.

It is possible to collect web statistics but they are notoriously unreliable in telling you how many people come to your site. The most reliable indicator is probably the number of distinct IP addresses visiting the site over a particular period, but even this is a long way from measuring the number of people or the number of 'visits'. In part this is a definitional problem (what do we mean by 'visit'?), but in part it is due to the way the Internet works at the moment. However, web statistics can be valuable if used with care. They can tell you which websites users came from to get to your site, showing how effective your link strategy has been. They can tell you which pages within your site are most popular, meaning you can restructure your site to feature content that is being missed or make popular pages easier to find. Log files can also tell you the search terms used on search engines that brought people to your site, allowing you to refine your site's metadata. If you have a search page within your site, analysis of popular searches and searches that produce no hits will tell you what people expect to find in your service. Make sure you provide opportunities for onsite feedback, include an e-mail address and a form that users can use to send feedback. If someone makes a complaint, learn from their frustration and try to change your site. If someone praises your efforts, it is always worth contacting them and asking if you can use their comments.

Top Tip
Marketing is a management process – evaluate it as such.

Marketing is both a management process and a set of practical tasks. Neglecting either is unlikely to be a route to success, however that is defined for your online information service.

Concluding remarks

Several of the case studies reported a relative undervaluing or even invisibility of the local information service (see Olaf, Chapter 7, and Peter, Chapter 3). The ongoing marketing challenge is to promote the information and credit for its availability without getting in its way.

Further reading

De Sáez, E.E. (2002) *Marketing Concepts for Libraries and Information Services*, 2nd edn. London: Facet.

Rowley, J. (2001) *Information Marketing*. Aldershot: Ashgate.

Special Libraries Association (1997) *Marketing Matters: An SLA Information Kit*. Washington, DC: Special Libraries Association.

16

Usability

Sarah Agarwal

'Usability' is a huge area. In academia, there are university departments dedicated to studying 'human–computer interaction' and there are nearly two million web pages containing the term 'usability' (*Google* search, December 2003). This chapter will give a general introduction to the subject as it relates to online applications and websites, and go over a few of the activities that readers could undertake on their own sites, with some enthusiasm and at little or no cost.

What is usability?

Most of us know what usability is because we have substantial experience of *unusable* websites that frustrate us and do not meet our requirements. For a more formal definition, Jakob Nielsen is one of the more approachable writers on the subject. He defines usability in five stages: Learnability, Efficiency, Memorability, Errors and Satisfaction (Nielsen, 2003). In summary, he says that a usable website is one where:

1. it is easy and quick to do whatever it is that the user came to the website to do (that is, their 'task');
2. it is easy to remember how to use it for future visits;
3. the user doesn't make many mistakes when they use the site, and any mistakes are easy to recover from;
4. the user gets subjective satisfaction from using the site.

Core Knowledge
Usability covers Learnability, Efficiency, Memorability, Errors and Satisfaction.

Usability needs to be addressed alongside content (see Chapter 13), because, even if a website is very easy to use, it won't be useful unless it contains the information that users require. Usability techniques are also used to help clarify content requirements.

Usability and accessibility (Chapter 16) are closely linked, though accessibility is more of a technical and ethical guidance framework for ensuring that all users can access the content of a site. In practice, an accessible site may tick all the boxes in terms of the guidance available, but it may still be unusable because of the way the navigation is set up, for example, or because it doesn't meet users' content requirements.

Why is it important?

Readers of this book are likely to be experienced Internet users, and each one of us can tell stories of websites which have frustrated and irritated us (for example, in Chapter 2, Sandeep tells of his frustration trying to discover directors' pay on company websites). Jared Spool researched the question, 'What percentage of the time are visitors successful at achieving their goals on the best-designed websites?', and the answer was 42 per cent (Spool et al., 1999). This means that more than half of visitors to the most usable websites go away disappointed. And, what's more, 40 per cent of visitors do not return to a site when their first visit was a 'negative experience' (Manning, McCarthy and Souza, 1998).

The implications of this are keenly felt in the e-commerce and private sector where poor usability results in lost revenue. However, for sites that may not exist with the main intention of turning a profit, the impact of poor usability can be harder to quantify and therefore easier to ignore. But, ultimately, the same principles apply for all website producers:

- If your intended users have difficulty using your site, they will go elsewhere.
- If you are the sole supplier of the information that's on your site, they may persevere, but their trust and perception of your organisation will diminish (Roy, Dewit and Aubert, 2001).
- You have (or will have) invested time and/or money in making your resources available online, so you want your customers to use them.
- Your customers' needs are central to the service you provide.

Additionally, with the advent of online information provision, the interface between the information provider and user has changed dramatically. Collections and resources are often laid bare to the user through the website and the information professional has little or no control (or even knowledge) of how successfully they are used. Within this context, usability becomes critical, as the web interface is frequently substituted for the reference interview. Instead of ensuring that users get the best information by providing it to them, information professionals must instead ensure that users can get easily to the appropriate information unaided by providing them with an interface that they find intuitive, effective and efficient.

There are two other points worth considering when making an early appraisal of whether usability is relevant to an online service. Firstly, a web producer who has not undertaken any usability analysis of his or her site often believes that it is easy to use. This is because they spend a lot of time using it, they understand the terminology used, they know where the key information is and, as a result of this familiarity, they are not able to see how other users could find it difficult to use. This doesn't imply that the interface is 'wrong' or 'bad', but it is a reflection of the producer's mind, not the customer's. If the producer agrees that customers' needs are central to the service, it follows that the interface should be user-centred.

Secondly, usability can be very cheap to do, much cheaper than any of the other aspects of web development. If at all possible, it makes sense to bring in a third party with expertise in the area to undertake usability activities, as the independence, skills and experience they bring will result in more and better quality results and, particularly, data interpretation and recommendations. However, significant improvements in usability can be achieved by individuals who are committed to understanding the usability of their sites who have done some reading on how to employ usability techniques. This is because any well-intentioned, open-minded interaction with users will be useful in understanding how the site can be modelled more closely to their requirements and perceptions, whether this be through user testing, requirements gathering or even through informal chats with users.

If all the above reasons are still not sufficient to convince managers to take usability seriously, they may be more impressed by the Standish Group research which found that user involvement is the most important element in delivering a successful project – more important than getting executive management support, financial issues or any of the other potential pitfalls that can blight a project (Standish Group International Ltd, 1994).

General guidelines

Various organisations have published guidelines for improving usability and these can be useful for web producers who are new to the topic and appreciate a simple checklist to compare their site with or to work from initially. These are some of the easily understandable ones, which are nevertheless supported by research:

- Sun Microsystems' 'Writing for the Web' guidelines can be used to ensure that users can read content on a site with ease (Nielsen, Schemenaur and Fox, 2002).
- Stanford Web Credibility Research has produced ten guidelines to ensure that websites are seen as credible and trustworthy (Fogg, 2002).

- The *National Cancer Institute* has lists of design guidelines, where each one is accompanied by an indication of the supporting research.
- The World Wide Web Consortium *W3C Web Accessibility Initiative*'s guidelines are frequently relevant to usability as well as accessibility, and are the standards recommended by the UK government. Ironically, however, they can be hard to understand.

However, all websites are different, and therein lie the severe limitations of relying on generic guidelines. Inevitably, at some point web producers have to get their hands dirty and involve their users.

Finding users

When doing any usability work with users, it may seem obvious to point out that the users should be representative of the target audience. In practice, a lot of developments and feedback mechanisms rely on informal groups of individuals who are known to the web producer, such as other managers and colleagues. It is essential to communicate with real users, as they are the only people who can reliably contribute the necessary data to enable the site to meet their requirements. This is particularly true at the requirements-gathering and specification stage.

If systems are being developed for in-house use, finding users is less of an issue. If users are external to the organisation, a little more effort may be needed. By far the easiest way of locating users is to go through communications previously received, such as e-mails, phone calls and visitors. Alternative sources can include professional and trade organisations, asking complementary organisations, posting to e-mail lists, asking local colleges and schools, and so on. It may be necessary to encourage users to take part by paying them a fee or, for surveys, entering them into a draw for a prize.

> **Top Tip**
> Usability information comes from real users, those who either do or will use the service.

The good news is that you only need between five and ten users to get the majority of the relevant data you need (Nielsen, 2000), so finding representative users need not be onerous. Once a relationship has been forged with users, this may prove fruitful for more than just usability testing.

Gathering users' requirements

Gathering users' requirements for a system is often seen as something that is done at the beginning of a project. While it is true that this is a critical time to document requirements, users' needs and expectations change and evolve (as do your competitors), so efforts to understand needs should be ongoing.

On many projects, the method of gathering user requirements for a system is often limited to a quick e-mail around a few individuals and some high-level discussions with senior managers. Politically, consultation with managers can be important. Yet, they are rarely the end-users of the system, and it is with the real users that a website will succeed or flounder.

There are many ways to gather requirements from users, including surveys, interviews, focus groups and observation. Whichever is used, the most useful data will be gathered by finding out users' goals and how they go about achieving these goals (Fuccella, Pizzolato and Franks, 1998), and then seeing how the website can or does help them achieve their goals. This is known as 'task analysis' and is seen by many usability professionals as the most important of all the usability techniques, for new or existing websites, because it describes the reality of users' goals and activities – the context in which the online resource needs to function. The case studies in this book in themselves provide valuable, if high-level, information to web producers about the context their site needs to work within. On the flip side, asking users, 'what would you like to have on the website?' won't help you as what users *say* they require is not necessarily what they will *use*.

The different techniques each have benefits and pitfalls, but for any of them to be successful, they need to be done with representative users.

Survey

This is a popular method as it's the easiest way to get round a lot of users and it can be a quick and easy way to find out quantitative information, such as how often users estimate they use certain sorts of information. It's less useful for finding out qualitative information, such as users' goals and activities, as the interpretation of survey questions and the analysis of results can lead to gulfs of misunderstanding. Even for quantitative surveys, questions have to be framed very carefully. For example, if you ask the question, 'Do you usually do a simple search on our site, or do you do an advanced search?', you are assuming the respondents know what you mean by these terms. Users may, in fact, believe that their searches are 'advanced' even though they don't use the Advanced Search feature. You don't need many misinterpretations of these questions to skew your results.

If surveys are run online, it's useful to be able to produce reports from the data without having to export it into another software package. Software such as BOS (*Bristol Online Surveys*) can do this.

Interview

Again, a representative sample of users needs to be interviewed, and the aim of the interview should be to understand users' current goals and activities as relevant to the website under study. Interviews are an excellent way of probing for more information, clarifying terms and identifying other issues that may be relevant. For a new development, the interview will particularly need to identify the environment in which the new site will need to function. For existing sites, this subject will still be relevant (particularly if it hasn't been investigated before), but the interview will also focus on how the site is used (or not!) to help the user achieve their goals. Interviewers need to be careful not to suggest answers to interviewees or to make assumptions about their requirements.

Focus groups

Gathering a representative group of users (or potential users) together can be a quick way to get an understanding of their requirements. As in the interview, the moderator needs to be careful not to lead participants or to make assumptions. Moderators also need to ensure that all participants have the time and opportunity to voice their opinions, and this is a particular issue for groups of participants who may not feel comfortable or confident giving dissenting opinions. Representative groups can be hard to gather together at one time.

Observation

This is by far the most effective yet, of course, the most expensive and time-consuming method. The observer spends some time in the user's environment noting activities and events. This gives a very real context and understanding of how the website is likely to be used or is currently used. In this situation, the observer does not need to rely so heavily on users reporting accurate information about their goals and activities as these can actually be viewed and recorded.

Informal chats

For those on a tight budget, or who are dipping their toes into the idea of making their website more user-centred, just having a few informal chats with users will prove useful and give an indication of the benefits that can be achieved by undertaking more in-depth usability work. Talking to users on an opportunistic basis, to discover how they use information and what for or how they use an existing site, will yield some excellent information. The feedback mechanisms on an existing site can also yield useful information, though neither of these methods are sufficiently robust to base decision-making upon.

For more information about techniques for gathering user requirements, try the advice from the *User-Centred Requirements Handbook* (Maguire, 1998).

Developing prototypes

Like a building, the success of a website depends on the strength of its foundations. Understanding users' requirements, goals and tasks gives this essential base from which to formulate ideas about how a site can be arranged and what content should be included to meet those requirements. From this point, ideas can be worked up into prototypes of a new, usable design.

The leap from understanding users' needs and goals to creating a new architecture is a huge and difficult one due to the complexities that are inherent in predicting new ways of doing things, which is basically what is happening when architectures are constructed. However, rather than worrying about how to construct a whole new system that will be usable and useful, it is much easier to construct some quick prototypes (which can be in HTML or on paper) of how the new site may work. These can be tested, iterated and retested with users in the same way that 'live' sites are tested.

Top Tip
Use low-tech prototypes to learn more about how people will use the service.

It is likely that a graphic designer will be employed to create the new prototypes. If so, the designer should be fully versed in the *W3C WAI Guidelines* and should have an understanding of, and empathy for, usable design. The UK government's *Quality Framework for UK Government Web Site Design* (Office of the E-Envoy, 2003) gives some good advice on how designers can be evaluated and how the commissioning process should work. More information and an example of paper prototyping can be found in the IBM technical library (for example, Snyder, 2001).

User testing

User testing is an effective way to find out how usable an existing site or prototype is. The most common way to carry out a test is to ask a group of users to complete a set of tasks on the website. This immediately raises the issue that the website producer needs to know what tasks and goals users commonly want to complete on the site, which in turn demonstrates how usability techniques work together – the tasks identified in the requirements-gathering phase can then be used to test against.

The importance of having valid tasks that users genuinely need to perform cannot be underestimated. After all, what is the value of testing to see if users can find the ISBN number of a book if they rarely want to do this? In addition to valid tasks which are specific to the website, other generic tasks should be tested such as finding contact names and numbers, finding directions and finding help.

Critically, the actual content of the site should be tested, not just the design and navigation. So, for example, you may have key documents on the site that contain statistics that you know from the requirements-gathering phase are important to users. In this case you should test how easily users can find the statistics rather than the document which contains them. Ultimately, it's the content within the pages that users want to reach, not the web pages themselves.

Several of the case studies in this book discuss issues around search effectiveness, and, if there is a search engine on the site, it should be evaluated alongside browsing to find out how successfully users find information, results are displayed and failed searches dealt with. The *National Cancer Institute Guidelines* list some of the search guidelines available, alongside an indication of the supporting evidence for each. Jared Spool's articles on the research that *User Interface Engineering* has done on searching are also interesting, helpful and easy to read.

Once the tests are complete, the results can be collated and the problems can be graded according to the impact they have on users' abilities to complete their tasks. This grading will help the web producer to prioritise where the redevelopment should focus.

Kupersmith (2003) has collated usability tests focusing on library terms that are commonly misunderstood by users. A clip of a usability test can be seen at the *Usability Sciences Corporation Usability Test Video Clip* site. Much useful information about how to conduct tests and interpret the results can be found at the *National Cancer Institute Usability* site.

Some other techniques

Heuristic evaluation

Web producers who are in the early stages of understanding and improving the usability of their sites often find that a 'heuristic evaluation' is a useful starting point. Here, a review of the site against a checklist of usability guidelines (Nielsen, 1994) is undertaken by two or more expert evaluators, who may apply extra custom heuristics depending on the nature of the site. Their evaluations are combined to give an overview of how well the site meets the checklist and recommendations are made to the web manager for improvement. Some samples from a heuristic review can be seen on the *Human Factors International* website.

Log analysis

Analysing search and other logs can indicate what users are looking for and how they are behaving on the site. Logs should be able to tell the web producer the route that a user takes through pages, which search terms have been used, how long they remain on a page, if they download anything, if they move to another site from links provided, and from which page the user leaves the system. This data can be used to build hypotheses about user behaviour. For example, if the logs show that users are not accessing one page at all, this could be because they can't find it, they are not interested in it or there is a technical problem reaching it. The web producer may then experiment by moving the page to a more visible part of the site or by renaming the link to it and then monitoring to see if it receives more visits. While these techniques are useful, they are no substitute for user consultation as they rely on a correct interpretation and solution being reached by the web producer, and they also give no information about users' tasks and goals. Jones, Cunningham and McNab (1998) offer an example of a log analysis for the New Zealand Digital Library.

'Competitive' review

Looking over the websites of organisations who provide similar or complementary information can give a web producer ideas of how they could evolve their site. Users can also be asked what they think of these sites, and this can be done by informal chats. If there is an opportunity for collaboration with complementary sites, the results of usability tests and evaluations can be shared (within the limits of the relevant data protection legislation – see Chapter 18). However, as each website is different, there are clearly limitations to the usefulness of this technique.

In conclusion

There are various stages in the development and lifetime of a website to which user involvement should contribute from the planning stage onwards. It's never too late or too early to seek user involvement. However, it is a fallacy to suggest that user involvement starts at the planning stage and ends once a review of the service or project has been completed. Dynamism is fundamental to websites, and even if the site doesn't change, the users' requirements certainly will.

The advent of Google changed the landscape of the web in terms of user interfaces. In user tests, the phrase 'Couldn't it be more like Google?' is frequently heard. The pressure is on for websites to perform in an intuitive, simple and efficient way, and this pressure is not going to evaporate.

Core Knowledge

Usability is no substitute for being customer-centred throughout the organisation.

Usability is not an effective alternative to having a truly customer-centred culture within an organisation, and an organisation which is not genuinely customer-focused is always going to struggle (and pay more!) to produce usable and well-received online offerings than an organisation which has a deep and intuitive understanding of its customers. Usability professionals are commonly asked to undertake usability activities on websites which show such fundamental misunderstandings of their users as to make the process of user involvement almost farcical. Examples include websites that disable the 'back' button or use splash screens or long *Flash* introductions to users who are clearly looking for quick, precise information, possibly from slow Internet connections, as many of the case studies in this book illustrate. Jared Spool's (2002) article *How Usability-Focused Companies Think* gives some excellent examples of the personality traits of companies who have a truly customer-centred approach to their business.

However, the majority of web producers understand that providing an online service that meets user requirements is a matter of success or failure, and, whatever their budget, utilising the usability techniques mentioned above will prove critical in the drive for quality, effectiveness and efficiency.

Further reading

Jakob Nielsen's website: *http://www.useit.com/*.

Office of the E-Envoy (2003) *Quality Framework for UK Government Web Site Design: Usability Issues for Government Web Sites*. Available at: *http://www.e-envoy.gov.uk/assetRoot/04/00/37/39/04003739.pdf*.

Spool, J., DeAngelo, T., Scanlon, T., Schroeder, W. and Snyder, C. (1999) *Web Site Usability*. San Francisco: Morgan Kaufmann.

17

Making your resource more accessible

Grace de la Flor and Andy Ramsden

Introduction

Chapter 12 suggested that a common theme from the case studies was the existence of barriers to accessing information. The nature and range of these barriers affects the degree to which the resource is accessible. The aim of this chapter is to raise awareness of accessibility in information professionals through answering the following questions;

1. What is web accessibility?
2. Why is it important for information professionals?
3. How can I make my material more accessible?
4. Where should I go for help?

What is web accessibility?

Letourneau (2003) defines accessibility as the ability for anyone using any kind of web browsing technology to visit any site and get a full and complete understanding of information contained there, as well as have the full and complete ability to interact with the site.

In practical terms, this means providing 'access to all' regardless of the type of device being used to access the content, the browser preference settings or any user disability, including low vision, hearing, motor skills or cognitive abilities. Even the use of low-grade technologies such as older operating systems, web browsers and dial-up modems must be taken into consideration when appraising the accessibility of online content.

> **Core Knowledge**
> Accessibility provides 'access to all' regardless of device, disability or technical limitation.

The case studies have tended to focus on the technical barriers to accessing the material, in particular the quality of the Internet connection. However, we also need to be aware that web-based resources need to account for a number of other issues. The benefits of developing accessible material are summarised by the *World Wide Web Consortium's (W3C) Web Accessibility Initiative* (WAI), who state that accessibility:

- helps ensure access to information for people with disabilities;
- provides greater usability for non-disabled web users;
- improves the technical performance of websites;
- shows an organisation's commitment to social responsibility.

Why is it important for information professionals?

From one perspective accessibility is important because information professionals are allocating a significant resource to developing web material to achieve a set of specific aims. However, the resources are wasted and the aims unachievable if the intended users cannot access the material. This point is evident from Olaf's case study, where it was found that some people could not access the resource because they did not have their browser configured with the appropriate plug-in software.

This problem becomes more acute as larger numbers of people look online for their primary sources of information. It is important to remember that the people who use your resource are not a homogenous group. Therefore your resource must accommodate a wide range of user characteristics or needs, including: people with disabilities, older people, people with low literacy levels, language (the resource may not be in the person's native language), low bandwidth and the use of older technologies. The need to account for these different characteristics is illustrated by the fact that 'there are 37 million people with disabilities in the EU, while the number of older Europeans is steadily increasing' (*European Commission: e-Accessibility: Web and People with Disabilities*).

In the wider context, making your web material more accessible is likely to make your resource comply with government legislation. There is a shift in legislation to ensure that all online material is accessible to all. This is evident in the UK with the Disability Discrimination Act (UK government, 1995) and Special Educational Needs and Disability Act or SENDA (UK government, 2001). Legislation to improve the accessibility of online material is being introduced in many jurisdictions, including the USA, the EU and Australia. A good starting point to identify current legislation by country is via the W3C *Web Accessibility Initiative* (WAI).

> **Top Tip**
> Find out what the legal responsibilities are for digital accessibility in your country.

How can I make my material more accessible?

It is not the intention of this chapter simply to list a set of technical specifications that, if adopted, will improve the accessibility of your resource. The aim is also to outline a strategy by which a developer can improve the accessibility of existing and new web material.

With respect to technical specifications, accessibility is primarily based upon technical solutions, such as the appropriate and valid HTML and cascading style sheets (CSS). The adoption of a few simple rules will enhance the accessibility of your resources; for instance, two of the case studies identified the existence of language barriers. A technical solution might include using the following HTML: `<HTML lang="it">` states that the primary language of the resource is Italian ('it'), while: `<span lang="fr"></span>` allows the inclusion of a different language (in this case French) within the text.

However, accessibility is not solely technical. For instance, the language barrier may be created by an inaccessible writing style. An important principle when designing material for onscreen reading is to remember that people process information in different ways. This implies that the developer needs to blend different presentational styles. For instance, if appropriate include:

- textual information;
- graphics;
- flow charts;
- lists;
- glossaries of terms and jargon;
- contents and index tables.

Table 17.1 summarises current good practice in using text to improve accessibility through enhancing onscreen readability.

One accessibility issue raised by the case studies was poor Internet connectivity. It is still evident that a large number of users have low bandwidth connections. In this situation, it is advisable to keep the file size to less than 70 kilobytes. This can be achieved by approriate design, clean HTML and the compression of images. You can also offer the resource in text-only format through the appropriate use of cascading style sheets (see the *W3C's Cascading Style Sheets Homepage*).

Table 17.1 Good practice in using text to improve readability

Colour schemes	Select a muted colour scheme in an attempt to reduce glare, while retaining enough contrast between the text and the background.
Lists	Use lists (bullets and numbers) as opposed to continuous prose. Numbered lists are preferable to bulleted lists.
Text	Use a single font type throughout the document. Don't emphasise large chunks of text and, when text is emphasised, use bold rather than italics or underlining. The ability to re-size text is important. Recommended typefaces include Arial, Verdana and Helvetica.
Paragraphs	All paragraphs should be left aligned. Try to aim for shortish paragraphs: around six to eight sentences per paragraph, and 40–65 characters per sentence.
Writing style	Write in short, simple sentences. State the aims and any instructions at the start of each page.
Pictures	Try to use pictures/images to break text into smaller chunks and provide a visual stimulus or memory trigger. However, try not to use flickering or moving pictures as these are distracting.
Overall	Try to maintain a common look and feel throughout your material. This helps the reader to become familiar with your style.

Top Tip

Try to predict technical barriers to information retrieval before delivering content to online users.

A strategy to improve the accessibility of a resource

You should implement an appropriate process to make your material more accessible. The following approach can be applied to both new and existing online material.

1. Identify a minimum acceptable accessibility benchmark for the resource.
2. Construct a checklist to ensure the material meets the acceptable benchmark.
3. Use both humans and automated tools to validate the accessibility of the resource.
4. Implement a clear and achievable project plan.
5. Draw up a clearly defined accessibility statement on your material.

These steps are described in more detail below.

Accessibility benchmarks

What standard should a web resource reach if it is to be classified as 'accessible'? An influential set of criteria for assessing the degree to which a resource is accessible has been developed by the *W3C Web Accessibility Initiative*. This has identified three levels of web accessibility compliance:

- *Priority 1.* A web content developer *must* satisfy this checkpoint. Otherwise, one or more groups will find it impossible to access information in the document. Satisfying this checkpoint is a basic requirement for some groups to be able to use web documents. Matching this priority will give your website a single 'A' rating.
- *Priority 2.* A web content developer *should* satisfy this checkpoint. Otherwise, one or more groups will find it difficult to access information in the document. Satisfying this checkpoint will remove significant barriers to accessing web documents. Matching this priority will give your website an 'AA' rating.
- *Priority 3.* A web content developer *may* address this checkpoint. Otherwise, one or more groups will find it somewhat difficult to access information in the document. Satisfying this checkpoint will improve access to web documents. Matching this priority will give your website an 'AAA' rating.

A minimum benchmark would be Priority 1 (rating: A). The following is an extract from the Priority 1 guidelines:

- Provide a text equivalent for all non-text elements.
- Ensure that all information conveyed with colour is also available without colour.
- Clearly identify changes in the natural language of a document's text and text equivalents (for example captions).
- Organise documents so they can be read without style sheets. For instance, when an HTML document is rendered without associated style sheets it must still be possible to read the document.
- Ensure that the equivalents for dynamic content are updated when the dynamic content changes.
- Avoid flickering screen images.
- Use the clearest and simplest language appropriate for a site's content.

From this extract it is evident that the approach is based on providing alternatives. The complete guidelines are available from the *W3C Web Accessibility Initiative* site.

> **Top Tip**
> Whatever your desired level of compliance it is important to test the accessability of the web resource with real users of your service – see Chapter 15.

Achieving the benchmark

After clarifying the degree to which your resource will be accessible, the next step is to write or rewrite your material to achieve this benchmark. A useful tool for improving accessibility is a checklist.

The checklist in Table 17.2 can be used to review existing web resources or as a reference point when developing new material. The checklist is divided into three sections:

1. Preliminary review – investigate how the resource renders under different browser settings.
2. Web content accessibility guidelines – investigate how the web resource validates against W3C WAI Priority 1 and 2.
3. Automated validation – investigate how the resource validates using automated tools, for instance HTML validation.

Table 17.2 Checklist for reviewing or developing a resource

Preliminary Review Browser tests – in Netscape and Explorer while adjusting the browser settings, conduct the following tests:		
Step	**Description**	**Comments**
A	Turn off images. Make sure that the information is presented in an appropriate sequence relative to the visual presentation.	
B	Turn off the sound. Make sure audio content is still available through text equivalents.	
C	Change the font size. Adjust to larger and smaller font sizes in the browser, and observe whether the page is still readable.	
D	Set the screen resolution. Test in 640 × 480 and 800 × 600 and ensure that this does not force the page into horizontal scrolling.	
E	Change the display colour. View page in black and white (or print out page on black and white printer) and observe whether colour contrast is adequate.	
F	Use tab keys. Put away the mouse and tab through the links and form controls on the page, making sure that you can access all links and form controls, and that the links clearly indicate what they lead to.	

Table 17.2 Continued

Conformance Evaluation Web Content Accessibility Guidelines 1.0 – validate the pages against Priority 1 and 2 W3C criteria:		
Step	**Description**	**Comments**
01	*Images and animations*. Use the ‘alt’ attribute to describe the function of each visual.	
02	*Image maps*. Use client-side image maps and alternative text for image map hot spots. If a server-side map is needed, provide equivalent text links.	
03	*Multimedia*. Provide captions or transcripts of important audio content. Provide transcripts or audio descriptions of important video content.	
04	*Hypertext links*. Use text that makes sense when read out of context. For example, avoid ‘click here’.	
05	*Page organisation*. Use headings, lists and consistent structure making visual layout clear.	
06	*Graphs and charts*. Summarise the content of each graph and chart, or use the `<longdesc>` element.	
07	*Scripts, applets and plug-ins*. When an applet, plug-in or other application is required to be present, provide a link to one that is directly accessible, or provide alternate content for those which are not directly accessible.	
08	*Frames*. Use the `<noframes>` element and meaningful titles for each frame.	
09	*Tables*. Make line-by-line reading sensible. Use the `<summary>` element.	
10	*Colour*. Don’t rely on colour alone to convey information. Ensure that text and graphics are understandable when viewed without colour.	
11	*Check work*. Validate using tools, checklists and guidelines.	

Table 17.2 Continued

Automated Evaluation Validate – run validation tools to test for compliance:		
Step	**Description**	**Comments**
I	*HTML validation*. HTML should pass validation. Performance outcome.	
II	*CSS validation*. Style sheets should pass validation. Performance outcome.	
III	*Bobby validation*. Report outcome.	
IV	*Lynx text browser*. Performance outcome.	
V	*Screen reader*. Performance outcome. Link text should make sense out of context, avoid phrases like 'learn more' or 'click here'.	

There are numerous checklists available on the Web. A good starting point is the *W3C's WAI Checkpoints*.

The validation of your material should involve a combination of both human and automated tools. The human validation tends to involve the use of the checklist and inspection of the code. The inspection of the code can be assisted by the use of automated tools, such as the *W3C MarkUp Validation Service*. These tools can validate the HTML or the CSS code. Alternatively, some software aims to evaluate the degree to which your material is accessible in terms of the Priority 1, 2 and 3 W3C WAI guidelines. Software such as *Bobby* scans your code and reports back on potential accessibility conflicts. The report structure maps the individual points within the WAI guidelines to your specific code. The report also provides linked information about the particular guideline. This link will include examples for contextualisation.

Automated validation tools have both strengths and weaknesses. The strengths include being able to quickly highlight potential accessibility conflicts. The weaknesses include the need for a human to review the report and decide whether the material is accessible based on the guidelines. For instance, the report may state, for example, 'User checks are triggered by something specific on the page; however, you need to determine manually whether they apply and, if applicable, whether your page meets the requirements.'

Generally, you should develop a strategy that efficiently incorporates the use of humans and automated tools within the validation process. For instance, the developer may create a set of templates that comply with accessibility standards. The pages may be marked up by different individuals and validated using the automated tools. The developer would then intervene when something unusual is encountered.

Implementing a project plan

An important part of the strategy is to write an achievable project plan for making your resource more accessible. This is especially important on existing resources, where it might appear quite daunting to implement accessibility compliance.

Part of the project plan might be to prioritise the order in which pages are addressed. For instance, start with the homepage then, based on the web access logs, focus on the most popular pages to the least popular. It is important to remember that all new pages should adhere to the required accessibility standard.

Top Tip

Prioritise your workload – remember the old saying, Rome wasn't built in a day!

(a) Home page and high-traffic pages
(b) All new pages
(c) Medium-traffic pages
(d) Longer-term goal of overall compliance.

You might also need to think about how you create your material. For instance, if you use a content management system, investigate if it can generate accessible code. On all types of content generation, try to ensure the appropriate use of CSS to separate content and visual presentation.

The following case study illustrates some of the issues involved in improving the accessibility of a web resource.

Case study

The Technical Advisory Service for Images website *(TASI)* was recently reviewed for its compliance to the Priority 1 guideline to bring it in line with SENDA (UK government, 2001), and as part of its application for inclusion in the UK's *National Grid for Learning*. The resource is between 150 and 200 pages which are manually maintained.

Antony Theobald, TASI's Technical Research Officer, outlined the process and some of the issues involved. The first stage was to manually check the site using the W3C's checklist for Priority 1. This process involved creating a list of all pages on the site by section and identifying all accessibility issues. The reason for the manual check was that the resource had recently been redesigned: the XHTML and CSS had already been validated using the W3C's automated tools, and it was felt that the automated accessibility checkers provided too much feedback. The review process highlighted four main issues:

- the need for support for PDF documents, in particular providing links to free viewers;
- the need for more informative 'alt' tag descriptions for images (for example, it was not acceptable to simply state 'Balloon' – more descriptive textual information was required);
- where 'alt' tags were not sufficient (for example, for complex flowcharts), HTML pages needed to be created as a text alternative, and the link to these had to be clearly identified;
- some data tables needed to be recoded to include the use of the 'scope' and 'header' tags.

Antony's view was that the project plan was well scoped in terms of its requirements and the time and resources needed. The lessons he learnt included:

1. Don't put it off – draw up a realistic and achievable plan. Opt for either a task or page approach (for example, 'I'll tackle all alt tags and then tables', or 'I'll start at the home page and work through the sections').
2. The process increased the whole team's awareness of the issues and highlighted the importance of consistency when developing accessible resources.
3. The process improved the site by making the team think about what it was trying to achieve and whether the material met these objectives.

Drawing up an accessibility statement

The final stage of the process is to draw up a clear accessibility statement for your resource. Many sites include an accessibility statement and a typical example can be found on the *Biz/ed* website. The accessibility statement should aim to:

- highlight the organisation's commitment to the issue of accessibility;
- include a clear named person(s) to contact if there are any questions concerning the accessibility of the resource;
- include information on how the developers have attempted to improve accessibility through the use of keyboard short cuts;
- advise on using assistive technologies with the resource.

> **Top Tip**
> Model your accessibility statement on those of other websites that you trust and respect, and always include a means for people to contact those responsible for the resource's accessibility.

Where should I go for help?

There is a significant amount of material available on the Internet with respect to accessibility. An important consideration is quality assurance and readability – in other words, is the source trusted and respected? Does it address your needs? The following list is not exhaustive but it is a good starting point.

Guidelines

W3C WAI Checklists of Checkpoints. Priority 1, 2 and 3 guidelines are included in this area. It includes checklists and techniques for developing accessible web pages:

- *http://www.w3.org/TR/WAI-AUTOOLS/atag10-chktable.html*
- *http://www.w3.org/TR/WAI-WEBCONTENT/full-checklist*

W3C WAI Developing Organizational Policies on Web Accessibility. This section of the W3C offers suggestions on how to implement an organisational web accessibility policy:

- *http://www.w3.org/WAI/EO/Drafts/impl/pol.html*

TechDis. UK resource centre supporting the further and higher education community in all aspects of technology and disabilities and/or learning difficulties:

- *http://www.techdis.ac.uk/*

Special Educational Needs and Disability Act (UK government, 2001). Read the actual legislation regarding the UK Disability Act:

- *http://www.hmso.gov.uk/acts/acts2001/20010010.htm*

UK Office of the e-Envoy Web Guidelines. This UK government office provides a useful website that includes a handbook on how to manage a website and a start-up kit that includes accessible HTML and CSS templates:

- *http://www.e-envoy.gov.uk/Resources/WebGuidelines/fs/en*

Tools

Watchfire WebXact. A free online service that lets you test single pages of web content for quality, accessibility and privacy issues:

- *http://www.webxact.com/*

HTML Validator. Provides an HTML validation service online:

- *http://validator.w3.org/*

CSS Validator. Provides a style sheet validation service online:

- h*ttp://jigsaw.w3.org/css-validator/*

Bobby Validator. A free service that tests web pages for barriers to accessibility, based upon the existing accessibility guidelines, such as Section 508 of the US Federal Rehabilitation Act of 1998, and the W3C's Web Content Accessibility Guidelines:

- *http://bobby.watchfire.com/bobby*

Lynx Browser. View a text-only version of web pages:

- *http://ugweb.cs.ualberta.ca/~gerald/lynx-me.cgi*

Homepage Reader. Test your pages using a text-to-speech reader web browser:

- *http://www-3.ibm.com/able/hpr.html*

BETSIE text-only parser. A filter program that creates a text-only version of your website:

- *http://www.bbc.co.uk/education/betsie/index.html*

VisCheck. Check web pages for how they would look to people with deuteranope (red/green), protanope (red/green), and tritanope (blue/yellow) visual colour deficits:

- *http://www.vischeck.com/vischeck/vischeckURL.php*

Adobe PDF accessibility. Adobe's website with resources for electronic document accessibility for people with disabilities such as blindness, low vision and motor impairments:

- *http://access.adobe.com*

W3C Evaluation Tools. This W3C web page has information regarding evaluation, repair and transformation tools useful for web content developers and web users who wish to make the Web more accessible:

- *http://www.w3.org/WAI/ER/existingtools.html*

W3C Alternative Web Browsers. A collection of pointers to information and, where possible, to demonstration versions of alternative browsing methods:

- *http://www.w3.org/WAI/References/Browsing*

Creating an accessibility statement. A 'how-to' for creating an accessibility statement for your website:

- *http://www.fixingyourwebsite.com/DiveIntoAccessibility/day_30.html*

Accessibility Bookmarklets. Useful tools to view your web pages for contrast compatibility, viewing without style sheets and testing HTML for alt tag inclusion:

- *http://www.508compliant.com/tools.htm*

Conclusion

It is both legally and ethically important to ensure that your online information service is accessible to all potential users. By describing how this can be done systematically and where you can go for further help, we hope we have shown that making your resource more accessible is a practical proposition. The overall message is that accessibility is good for all your users and, while the process may seem daunting, it can be achieved by breaking it down into smaller chunks and allocating resources for an appropriate timescale.

Acknowledgements

We wish to acknowledge Dr Kieren Pitts, the Senior Technical Researcher at *Biz/ed*, for his valued comments on this chapter.

18

Legal issues

Christine Mullings

Note: The aim of this chapter is to offer useful tips to those running online information services. However, nothing in this chapter should be taken as legal advice, and it is recommended that readers consult a qualified professional in the event of any query.

Introduction

This chapter looks briefly at three important legal issues that are likely to confront information professionals: data protection, freedom of information and intellectual property. In this short space, there can be no definitive statements or extended discussion of any of these issues. I have therefore limited the aim to merely sketching each domain and providing some pointers as to where to find further information.

The focus of the chapter is on the situation in the UK, although the nature of global networks means both that international factors are of increasing relevance and that some aspects of the legal context are becoming similar across jurisdictions. For up-to-date information, the best place to monitor is probably the *Keeping Legal* site.

Data protection

This is important for anyone holding personal information about others, for example staff, students, patients, users, research subjects. The UK Data Protection Act of 1998 (UK government,

1998) succeeded the 1984 Act. In the Act, personal information can be any information about a living individual that might identify them, for example a postcode, National Insurance number, National Health Service number, telephone number and so on. The Act applies to all records kept, whether on paper, electronically, recordings, photographs or audio/videotape. It states that individuals have a right to see what data is held on them, and that they be given a chance to rectify any information that is wrong. Also, the data must be held for specific and lawful purposes and only disclosed to the individual concerned, not passed on to others without seeking the individual's permission.

Core Knowledge
Data protection legislation may apply to both electronic and paper documents; you need to check the rules within your jurisdiction.

Questions that you need to address are:

- What data do you hold?
- Are they accurate?
- Where are the data stored?
- Are they held securely?

Examples where data protection legislation may be relevant

Databases

Regard (which is the *Economic and Social Research Council*'s online database of research in the social sciences) holds details of research grants awarded and research outputs produced. Most of the information held is publicly available on the website and can be checked by anybody at any time. However, in addition, personal contact details such as addresses, telephone numbers and e-mail addresses are held out of the public view to enable ease of contact between the service and the grant holders. To comply with the Data Protection Act we issue a statement to award holders at the start of their contract to inform them that we will not release contact details to other parties without their prior permission. In addition we 'survey' them on a regular basis to check that the personal data we hold on them is accurate and up to date. We then amend our records accordingly. We also try to ensure that we only hold one copy of this information centrally to avoid the mistakes that duplicate information can lead to. Data such as these should always be stored on a secure server and not on an individual's hard disk.

E-mail archives

Projects or services may set up an e-mail address so that users can contact the service with problems/queries. These e-mails are often stored in archival form and are accessible to members of the team. They must always be restricted to team use only and there should be a statement on the project website informing users that their e-mails and contact details will be stored this way. The *Regard Data Protection Statement* includes a passage on this topic.

Registration information

Some projects or services require a user to register before obtaining access to certain levels of information. Data acquired this way are held locally and are available to the team. Again, a statement needs to be made to users that data are collected and stored in this way, what they are used for and what an individual's rights are. For all password-protected data, passwords should never be disclosed. The Social Science Information Gateway's *SOSIG Privacy Statement* is a relevant example.

Research data

Projects or services may collect data (for example, in conducting usability research) by interview, questionnaire, focus groups and so on. Sometimes these data may be recorded on audio or videotape. Permission must be sought to record data. Tapes should be transcribed as soon as possible and then wiped clean and transcripts should only be kept for as long as necessary. Individuals should be anonymised in transcripts. Names should be stored separately from other data and ID codes used instead. Many research ethics codes specify these requirements in detail, for example that of the British Psychological Society (2000).

Sensitive data

Be especially careful with 'sensitive' data and question the need to collect/keep them. With this kind of data you need special permission from the subject to collect the data. Examples of this kind of data are racial categories or political opinions, information about physical or mental health and criminal acts, and 'politically sensitive data' such as that relating to human cloning. Images can be sensitive data, for instance those taken during medical treatment, and consent to hold and display them must be obtained. The *Bristol Biomed* service has considerable experience in these matters. Finally, databases on patients may also be deemed 'sensitive'.

Freedom of Information Act 2000

Freedom of information varies dramatically between countries, from the rights-based approach in the United States to hitherto rather less open regimes such as that of the UK. The UK Freedom of Information Act (UK government, 2000) covers all public authorities in England, Wales and Northern Ireland such as local and central government, the police, the NHS, schools and universities. It gives citizens a statutory right of access to many kinds of recorded information for the first time. By January 2005, full rights to request information come into force and authorities will have to deal with requests for disclosure. The Act will place a new focus on information retrieval in the public sector, although there are many exemptions to disclosure, especially relating to policy information.

The Act has the potential to transform the relationship between society and government in terms of transparency and openness, leading to more dialogue and informed policy- and decision-making. There is a target that all government records should be managed electronically by 2004, leading to a major new emphasis on records management, with the *Public Records Office Records Management* site offering a useful overview of UK public initiatives in this field. It looks as though many organisations will combine their implementation of responsibility for data protection and freedom of information.

The Act will mandate the introduction and maintenance of 'publication schemes', that is descriptions of what information a public authority publishes or intends to publish and whether this will be available free of charge or on payment. Examples include the *UK Ministry of Defence Publication Scheme* and the *Economic and Social Research Council Publication Scheme.* However, not all publication schemes are easy to locate – for example, many local authority schemes are not well advertised.

An article in *FreePint* by Stephen Wood (Wood, 2003) gives plenty of background to the Act including the timetable for implementation, publication schemes and some further implications.

Intellectual property

Of the three legal issues covered in this chapter, it is intellectual property that featured most strongly in the case studies. Jeremy, Annabel and Olaf all noted (or failed to note!) the restrictions that copyright law puts on their use of information. Copyright law is constantly undergoing revision, but rapidly changing technology in terms of electronic publishing tends to run faster than the legislation. The basic concepts of copyright law still apply to electronic documents but can be difficult to enforce. Once a work is in electronic form, copies can be made and distributed on a global scale only too easily and there seems to be much greater potential for exploitation. On the other hand, there is also a much greater potential for control. Professor Lawrence Lessig of Stanford University has noted that '[Creativity] has never been more controlled in our history – ever' (Thompson, 2003). Certainly it would appear that there is a general trend toward a much more restrictive regulatory regime than we are used to, as manifested in the US Digital Millennium Copyright Act (US government, 1998), and in the EU Copyright Directive (European Parliament and Council, 2001), and managed under the auspices of the *World Intellectual Property Organisation* (WIPO, 1996). The key thing for the information professional to know is that what the technology allows and disallows often bears little relation to what the law allows and disallows.

Core Knowledge

What the technology allows and disallows often bears little relation to what the law allows and disallows.

It would be pointless to try to summarise such a vast, fast-moving and deeply contested topic as copyright. Hence much of this section is devoted to an annotated list of pointers to web resources that should be more up to date than a book could ever be.

The situation in the UK and the EU

In the UK at present, copyright is determined by the Copyright, Designs and Patents Act 1988 (CDPA) (UK government, 1988), and the principle is that the original intellectual property is 'owned' by the creator of the work, be it literary, musical, sound recording or software. Permission is needed from the owner for any reproduction or adaptation of the original work. Types of materials may include text, still images, moving images, sound, educational media and websites. However, typically, the creator transfers the copyright to a publisher or similar body. Some materials are then licensed for use under certain conditions, and copying may be permitted by the *Copyright Licensing Agency* (CLA), for example for photocopying by library users, although certain regulations are set down. The effects of the CDPA are being revised by the introduction of the EU Copyright Directive (European Parliament and Council, 2001), which is introducing a somewhat stricter regime, with a smaller tolerance of traditional 'fair dealing' exemptions than UK professionals are used to. In particular, it will be illegal to circumvent technological measures imposed by copyright owners to restrict use of material, even where a person has a right to use the material. Further information on the implementation process of this legislation is available from Brown (2003) or from *Eblida ECUP* (European Copyright User Platform), which deals with copyright problems related to electronic information, whose website includes a list of projects running under the scheme. The UK situation is covered by the *Keeping Legal – Copyright* section, or by the *Libraries and Archives Copyright Alliance.*

The situation in the US

The new, stricter copyright regime is in place in the US. A first place to look for resources is *Berkeley Digital Library Copyright*, which includes a quick bibliography as well as sections on current awareness, organisations, articles, papers and reports, and laws, politics and court opinions. For an expert defence of people's freedoms in the digital age, the best place to look is the *Lessig Blog* by Professor Lawrence Lessig.

New initiatives in intellectual property rights (IPR)

Many non-profit organisations are making literature freely available, such as e-print archives, which usually include electronic full-text and metadata of research outputs. The *Open Archives Initiative* develops and promotes interoperability standards for e-print archives. However, there are potential copyright problems where people publicly archive their own copies of material that they may have authored but that has been commercially published and where the copyright has been transferred to the publisher. In the academic world, a precedent may have been set within the physics community, with their *Arxiv* resource, and there are strong advocates for working within the current copyright framework to achieve greater access to, particularly academic research, material (Harnad, 2001). The position of academic publishers on this topic varies and is summarised in the '*RoMEO*' table, now maintained on the *SHERPA* site.

However, some are now questioning whether copyright is the best route forward and whether other expressions of IPR might be appropriate. From the technical point of view, the W3C (1997) some time ago drafted an overview of copyright and Internet technologies. From the social point of view, the UK government in 2001–2 set up a *Commission on Intellectual Property Rights* to look into how IPR might work better for poor people and developing countries. It concluded that 'intellectual property systems may, if we are not careful, introduce distortions that are detrimental to the interests of developing countries' (Commission on Intellectual Property Rights, 2002). These and other drivers (for example, the open source software movement discussed in Chapter 22) have led to new expressions of intellectual property, often based around licensing. For example, *Creative Commons* offers a set of 11 licence agreements by which authors can make their material available with different levels of rights for the user but without relying on copyright protection. Even more radically, from the open source software movement comes the idea of *Copyleft*, whereby software is made freely available on the condition that it and developments of it are also made freely available.

Concluding remarks

In terms of running an online service, perhaps the most useful tip is to consult the many advisory services available, such as the *JISC*

Legal Information Service in the UK, perhaps the EU *Intellectual Property Rights Helpdesk* on Europe-wide issues and the *US Department of Justice Computer Crime and Intellectual Property Section* on US law and practice. The situation is fluid, with information professionals taking an active role in both defending access to information and protecting creators.

Further reading

Cornish, W.R. and Llewelyn, D. (2003) *Intellectual Property: Patents, Copyright, Trade Marks and Allied Rights*, 5th edn. London: Sweet & Maxwell.

Davison, M.J. (2003) *The Legal Protection of Databases*. Cambridge: Cambridge University Press.

Stamatoudi, I.A. and Torremans, P.L.C. (eds) (2000) *Copyright in the New Digital Environment: The Need to Redesign Copyright*. London: Sweet & Maxwell.

19

Building user skills

Neil Jacobs

Introduction

The case studies making up the first part of this book suggest that users feel that they have the information skills they need to do their work. What else would they say? However, both professional experience and the results of research suggest that end-users often lack something from the professionals' toolkit that would make their use of resources either more efficient or more effective (see, for example, Martin and Rader, 2003). Increasingly, it is the role of the information professional to keep her or his own skills comprehensively up to date, and to ensure that relevant subsets of these are effectively transferred to end-users.

We conclude this book by looking at the changing role of the information professional, and one aspect of these changes (which parallels similar changes elsewhere, for example in the role of teachers and lecturers within education) is this shift from gatekeeper of authoritative knowledge to coach and adviser supporting independent end-users. The challenge is to convince users that they will waste more time and money by not having information skills than they will save by not working to acquire them.

The case studies do confirm that this is a challenge – many users do think they are managing. Partly, this is about marketing (see Chapter 15). If a part of the online service being offered is skills transfer, then that needs to be made explicit, that this is a package and the web pages are only a part of the deal. This case can only be made convincingly from a detailed knowledge of what your end-users are doing. But it also requires a good understanding of what kinds of skills might be relevant, and therefore how to identify a need that the user will recognise as important. In this chapter, I will describe what kinds of skills might be relevant to users of online services, and run through a range of these in a little detail.

User skills: what are they?

Information skills are typically undervalued, both by those who have them and by those who don't. One reason for this may be that many users (including most of the case studies in this book) are self-taught and therefore have had little opportunity to reflect on what they have learned and what they might still have to learn. Another reason for the undervaluing of information skills is that they are rarely spelt out in any detail (but see Grayson and Gomersall, 2003). Too often, they are summed up in short phrases that sound like little more than common sense. However, detailed descriptions of what we mean by 'information skills' have been produced, notably in the UK by *SCONUL* (Society of College, National and University Libraries), in Australia by *CAUL* (Council of Australian University Librarians) and in the US by the *ACRL* (Association of College and Research Libraries). These and others have been usefully compared by the UK *Big Blue Project* in a taxonomy of user skills that is shown as Figure 19.1.

Once set out like this, it seems clear that information skills do, in fact, involve high-level cognitive functions such as evaluation, synthesis and classification. In presenting the value of these skills to users, and asking them to give up time and even money to learn about them, using this kind of language and framework can help ensure that the skills are taken seriously. It can also help overcome what the Further Education lecturer (Chapter 3) called 'institutional inertia', which prevents the embedding of ICT use into organisational practice. Users and institutions both have plenty of other things they could be spending their time and money on, and information skills training needs to compete successfully with these other calls on resources.

Core Knowledge
Information skills are not just common sense; they can be described in a clear framework that emphasises their coherence.

In the remainder of this chapter, we will look at information skills and how each one can be demonstrated to be important to users.

Specification

Specifying the topic of a query can be straightforward, but it is often less straightforward than it at first appears. For example, someone may be looking for figures for the costs of providing ambulances to take older people to hospital, but have they considered existing research into this issue, or comparative figures for not using ambulances (using taxis, for example), or evidence of other benefits or costs associated with this use of ambulances? Clearly, information professionals may find themselves in difficult positions if they imply that users have got the question wrong, but that is the negotiation that reference librarians have been undertaking for a long time. The first skill a user needs is to be able to specify a question that is most relevant to their project and is answerable within the resources they have available to them. As Annabel notes (Chapter 9), the skills of the reference interview are still important. Of course, the user may not be in a position to 'question the question'; they may merely have been asked to gather such-and-such intelligence. Nevertheless, the user is interested in making a defensible approach to the question asked, and this is a skill that can be learned. In many ways, it is similar to the skill in defining a practical research question. A specification checklist, derived from one used to help students define a practical research question, is as follows:

1. Explore around the topic – get a feel for where it fits with neighbouring topics, and for what the main issues are.

Figure 19.1 Taxonomy of information skills

Information skills/competency standards		United States				Australia		United Kingdom
		ACRL (2000)	Doyle (1992)	Dupuis (1997)	Rader (1996)	CAUL (2000)	Bundy (2001)	SCONUL (1990)
	Skill 1	**Determines** the nature and extent of information needed	**Recognises** the need for information **Recognises** that accurate and complete information is the basis for intelligent decision-making	**Articulate** when and what information is needed	**Formulate** and **analyse** information needs	**Recognises** need for information and **determines** the nature and extent of information needed	**Recognises** a need for information	**Recognises** a need for information
	Skill 2		**Identifies** potential sources of information	**Select** appropriate tools or sources and search effectively	**Find** resources for identified information needs Select resources for identified information needs	**Accesses** needed information effectively and efficiently	**Determine** the extent of the information needed	**Distinguish** the ways of addressing the information gap
	Skill 3	**Accesses** needed information effectively and efficiently	**Develops** successful search strategies		**Identify** and **appraise** the value of the source Evaluate the information searching process	**Evaluates** information and sources **critically** and incorporates into knowledge base and value system		**Construct** strategies for locating information
	Skill 4		**Access** sources of information including computer-based and other technologies		**Record** and **store** information	**Classifies, stores, manipulates** and **redrafts** information collected or generated	**Access** the needed information efficiently **Access** and **use** information **ethically** and **legally**	**Locate** and **access information**
	Skill 5	**Evaluates** information and its sources **critically** and incorporates selected information into his or her knowledge base and value system	**Evaluates** information	**Evaluate** materials across mediums and formats		**Expands, reframes or creates new knowledge** by integrating prior knowledge and new understandings as an individual or member of a group	**Evaluate** the information and its sources **critically**	**Compare** and **evaluate** information obtained from different sources

Information skills/competency standards	Skill 6	Individually or as a member of a group, **uses** information effectively to accomplish a specific purpose **Understands** many of the **economic, legal** and **social** issues surrounding information use and accesses and uses information ethically and legally	**Organises** information for practical application	**Manipulate** and **organise** the information retrieved **Communicate** to others the location and content of information found	**Present** and **communicate** findings **Interpret, analyse, synthesise** and **evaluate** collected information	**Understands cultural, economic, legal** and **social** issues surrounding information use and accesses and uses information ethically and legally	**Incorporate** selected information into knowledge base **Use** information **effectively** to accomplish a purpose **Classify, store, manipulate** and **redraft** information collected or generated **Understand economic, legal, social** and **cultural** issues in the use of information	**Organise, apply** and **communicate** information to others in ways appropriate to the situation
	Skill 7		**Integrates** new information into existing body of knowledge			**Recognises** that lifelong learning and participative citizenship require information literacy		**Synthesise** and **build** on existing information, **contributing** to the **creation of new knowledge**
	Other skills		Use information in **critical thinking** and **problem solving**				**Recognise** information literacy as a prerequisite for lifelong learning	

Source: Big Blue Project.

Of course, these are very generic skills, and will be interpreted differently in each sector. In terms of further education (FE), for example, the Scottish Further Education Funding Council has published a training needs analysis in ICT for the Scottish FE sector in 2001 (SFEFC, 2001). Their findings echo Peter's experience (see Chapter 3), in that there is generally widespread use of tools such as word processing, e-mail and the Internet but that there is a lack of skills required to use ICT in an active way to deliver learning or assessment to students, and that the barriers are lack of time and lack of institutional support. The training needs identified were:

- awareness-raising of the potential benefits of online learning;
- evaluating online learning materials;
- creating online courses;
- communication – online discussion, tutoring, video conferencing;
- updating basic skills.
- sourcing online learning materials;
- pedagogy in an online environment;
- designing online assessments;
- basic skills – support for European Computer Driving Licence;

There is potentially a role for information professionals within the sector to get involved in these training requirements.

2. Look at the topic from a number of perspectives (perhaps economic, social, environmental...), and consider what questions other people are asking about it.
3. Consider the scale of the information involved – if it is too large then it may need to be more tightly defined.
4. Consider the scope of the information required – does it need to be up to date, does it have to be peer-reviewed, and so on.
5. Check whether the information sources are accessible to provide the information required.
6. Identify criteria that will tell you when you have answered the question.

Finally, the user will need to be reflective about their role in the process. For example, if they are working in a policy environment, then perhaps they have been brought in at a late stage in the policy development process to lend support to a policy whose main parameters have already been set. Or perhaps the user is marketing the information they find as a product to a client. For example, Sandeep in the trade union researcher case study clearly knew very well how the information he was asked for would be used and defined his need accordingly. In short, users can be in any of a number of positions and need to reflect on this position in order to specify their information requirement properly. Information professionals need to demonstrate that they understand this.

Identifying sources

Once the information requirement has been specified, then the user needs to use imagination and skill in deciding which sources will best answer it. Of course, you may already have done some selection work for the user (see Chapter 13) in drawing together high-quality, relevant sources (books, databases, web sources and tools). However, each query will need a different set of sources. Again, this is not as straightforward as it may seem. If we think again of transporting older people to hospital, then should the user look for transport sources, health sources or age-related sources? Research evidence alone appears in different places according to whether it is ongoing, just completed or has been peer-reviewed, and is produced by a myriad of bodies including universities, think-tanks, governments and others. The range of sources is correspondingly large (databases, websites, library catalogues, newsletters and so on). The challenge here is to overcome the view that everything (or enough) is on the surface Internet, as several of the case studies seemed to assume. It may be necessary to use the staggering statistic that well over 99 per cent of the publicly available material on the Web is the so-called 'deep Web', hidden within databases and inaccessible to standard search engines (Bergman, 2001).

> **Top Tip**
> Respect Google (as your users do), but be able to show why and how it is not enough.

Evaluating sources

Evaluation needs criteria, and the criteria for evaluating information sources depend on both the information need and the type of source. In terms of formal databases, it pays to look at:

- the extent of the information held (contact details, full text);
- the formats in which it is available;
- subject coverage;
- document coverage (grey literature, peer-reviewed papers);
- currency;
- indexing (searching is more effective where databases are properly indexed and a controlled vocabulary is available – see Chapter 20);
- searching (basic or sophisticated Boolean, phrase, intelligent searching);
- cost.

Where the source is not a formal database, it may be just a website. If anything, the case studies suggested that this is often the typical situation. The user will have to work harder to assess the potential value of a website. Furthermore, websites vary in their scope both between sites and across time (the same site will be different the next time a user visits it). Some guidance is available from the *Virtual Training Suite*, and the basic approaches are:

- Check the metadata – is there information about the author, the coverage, the version, the frequency with which the site is updated?
- Check the authors – can evidence be found that they are respectable, have they published in well-known publications?
- Check the site sponsor or host – is it a university or other reputable site? Is the sponsor trying to sell something?

> **Top Tip**
> Advise users to decode the URL – it contains clues about the provenance and likely quality of a web resource.

Finally, for Internet sites, it is always worth decoding the URL. An Internet address, such as *http://www.bris.ac.uk/depts/PathAndMicro/staff/smith.html* contains clues as to its provenance. In this case, *www.bris.ac.uk* suggests that this is a UK university *.ac.uk*, and is probably Bristol *bris*. As for the rest of the address, *depts/PathAndMicro* suggests a university department (Pathology and Microbiology), and *staff/smith* suggests that this is a member of staff's page, whose name is Smith.

Where this address contains the suffix *.ac.uk*, other addresses might have:

- *.edu* – university in the US;
- *.co.uk* or *.com* or *.net* – commercial site or site hosted by commercial Internet service provider (this includes many third-sector organisations, as well as for-profit companies);

- *.org* – not-for-profit organisation that has sufficient expertise and/or money to acquire its own domain name;
- *.gov* – government body.

Building a strategy

This is not the place to explain the nuts and bolts of building a search strategy, the use of Boolean and phrase searching, identifying synonyms, using thesauri, iterative searching and so on. It is worthwhile, though, for an information professional to consider the different conventions used by the sources that most users will search. For example, the level of Boolean searching supported, the characters used for wildcards (and their rules of application), and the conventions for phrase searching may all vary between sources, so users may find it useful to have a single place with all these conventions spelt out. Until effective cross-searching of any set of sources from a single interface becomes a reality on the ground, then users will need to be aware of how these conventions vary.

Evaluating the information

Of course, once the user has a results set and has obtained the relevant documents, he or she needs to evaluate which are relevant and of high quality. This is different to evaluating the information sources and refers to the documents themselves. There are some principles that are widely applicable, drawn from the research methodology literature. If we consider a particular policy report, for example, these principles may be summarised as:

1. *Reliability.* This refers to consistency, that is is the report consistent in the way it uses other documents, or does it seem to prefer some over others for no obvious reason?

2. *Validity*. This is concerned with whether the report is really about what it claims to be about (for example, perhaps its title or abstract is misleading), and whether it is about the topic in which the user is interested.
3. *Ethics*. Put simply, the user should ask themselves whether the report was compiled ethically, with appropriate consent from or citation of those quoted.
4. *Systematicity*. By this I simply mean that the report should be written in a systematic way, clearly showing how any recommendations were reached and so on.
5. *Credibility*. The report should be from a credible source, that is a source that will be respected by those whom the user is trying to inform.
6. *Transparency*. Does the report contain sufficient information for the user to decide on points 1–5?

Once the user has evaluated the information and found it to satisfy all of these criteria, then she or he is in a position to use the information. Of course, the user may not see it as the information professional's role to advise on the quality of the information found. Again, the key is to demonstrate that the skill is worth having and is not common sense!

Using the information

It may seem superfluous to include a section on using the information but the information professional may have skills to pass on here too. For example, there is a variety of ways in which information can be brought together (Jackson et al., 2000). These include tracing the history of a particular topic, categorising the work done according to some taxonomy, undermining the apparent consensus on a topic and synthesising information into a new whole. Depending on what the user is trying to achieve, any one or more of these may be appropriate strategies. And then there are the practical issues concerning plagiarism, proper citation and the format and level of any report the user might write based on the information found.

Summary

A user skills programme is a vital component of any online information service, often especially where users consider themselves not to need such a programme. To persuade users of the value of information skills, it can be useful to have some anecdotal 'horror stories' demonstrating what happens when information is missed or the need is misinterpreted or the information is misused. Another tactic is to work through your organisation's existing staff development and training programme, since information literacy is increasingly seen as a key transferable skill that benefits both employer and employee. Once the user is convinced of the benefits of acquiring information skills, then they should be presented systematically, perhaps showing how they fit into a coherent framework. This, again, will help to persuade users that the skills are not merely common sense. The programme itself will need to be tailored to the needs of particular users, but may include some of the elements described in this chapter on specifying the need, identifying and evaluating sources, and evaluating and using information. While online tutorial options are a possibility, if used alone they can eliminate the valuable marketing and intelligence-gathering opportunity offered by face-to-face sessions, however difficult these are to arrange.

Further reading

Macoustra, J. (2003) 'Information literacy in a corporate environment', *FreePint*, no. 132. Available at: *http://www.freepint.com/issues/060303.pdf*.

Martin, A. and Rader, H. (eds) (2003) *Information and IT Literacy: Enabling Learning in the 21st Century*. London: Facet.

20

Subject classification

Paul Ayres

What is classification and why do it?

Subject classification is the act of adding subject headings to records, documents, web pages or other media in a consistent and organised manner. The aim of classification is to help users retrieve information that is appropriate to their needs (as Annabel notes – see Chapter 9). While the most common manifestation of this may well be in terms of helping users when they input a query into a search box on an electronic service, it also has many other uses. Given that users of electronic services like to browse resources as well as search for specific items, a good subject classification scheme can be reused as the backbone of a website or service allowing users to access it by subject-specific sections dedicated to particular topics. A good subject tree can also be used as a basis for information push services; for example, a user (such as Jeremy in Chapter 6, for instance) may wish to sign up for e-mail-based alerts about specific topics covered within your service. Allowing users to set their preferences to e-mail updates about specific subjects will allow them to cope with potential information overload and give them more focused, meaningful information. Classification should aim to make a body of resources manageable, easily comprehended and navigable in a logical manner.

How to classify

In order to classify resources effectively you need to decide upon a scheme to use. The choice of scheme will depend upon your circumstances, the needs of your user base, the resources that you have available and the limitations of the technical system within which you are working. A number of standard universal schemes exist, the most common of which include the *Library of Congress Classification* (LOC) scheme, the *Dewey Decimal Classification* (DDC) scheme and the *Universal Decimal Classification* (UDC) scheme. These schemes are characterised by being broadly based, relatively stable and slow to change. They are suitable for resources that cover a very large range of material that reflects all of human experience.

However, your service may be focused on a single subject area where a very general classification scheme will not go into enough detail and will also contain much superfluous content which you will never need to use. In this case, it is worth exploring the subject-specific classification schemes that relate to your service, for example resources working in the field of psychology should consider the *American Psychological Association* (APA) scheme as a possibility for subject classification. Subject-specific schemes are characterised by being highly detailed, often long established and focused on academic or scholarly environments. They are particularly useful when you know that you will be serving a particular user community, members of which share a common way of looking at things.

While space considerations mean we cannot consider all possible schemes for all possible subjects with the social sciences, some basic research should lead you towards an appropriate subject scheme soon enough. You may have a subject classification scheme mandated to you due to the nature of the organisation within which you work, or the fact that you serve a particular sort of client who you know may search for items in a certain way. For example, those working within central government in the United Kingdom should be aware of, if not already using, the *Government Category List* as a classification scheme. Such lists are characterised by being accessible to a wide range of users, up to date with current terms and subject to regular updating. However, their flexibility and up-to-the-minute applicability mean that they may not be suitable for resources which you know will have a long lifetime or if you only have a very limited amount of time to devote to subject classification, as they may need updating.

You may even decide to create your own classification scheme. This may seem like a good idea, as it will closely reflect the needs of your organisation and should be able to be changed relatively easily. However, there are drawbacks. Developing a home-grown scheme is a time-consuming process, even if you have subject and information specialists to call on. While the scheme may reflect your thinking, it may not reflect the views of the broader organisation, or may just be unfamiliar to them. Finally, it will be difficult to interoperate with other schemes or systems, which can be of vital importance.

> **Top Tip**
> Before building your own scheme, ask whether an established one wouldn't work just as well, and be more familiar to your users.

Controlled vocabularies and browsing

As well as assigning a subject classification to parts of your service, another practice to aid retrieval of items within it is adding keywords to individual records or texts. For example, while you may use your subject classification scheme to assign an item to the broad area of 'Social Policy' and the subsection of 'Housing Policy', you may also add keywords like 'homelessness', 'rough sleepers' or 'begging' to help users find that item. The keywords you use should be chosen from a controlled vocabulary, that is a list of words within an overall scheme, to allow consistency and provide a way of retrieving all items relating to a specific topic. You can develop and use your own scheme of keywords, but bear in mind that this contains many of the same potential pitfalls that developing your own subject classification scheme can have. You may choose to use one that already exists; for example, the HASSET scheme (*Humanities and Social Science Electronic Thesaurus*) has been developed by the *UK Data*

Archive specifically for describing academic social science research. The *Library of Congress Subject Headings* (LCSH) listing covers a much broader spectrum of experience, but is widely used within the library and information world.

Whether you use an existing scheme or develop your own, all such keyword schemes need to have various facilities, for example 'preferred terms' or 'see' references, where it is made clear that if you are looking for, say, 'fishing' then the term used in the keyword list is 'angling' (see Barbara's account in Chapter 11). Users may well wish to broaden or narrow their search when they get results relating to a particular enquiry, so an enquiry into UK examinations may have a narrower term linked to it for GCSEs or A-levels, and a broader term such as pupil assessment or curriculum studies.

A subject classification scheme cannot be seen in isolation. Indeed, you may want to interoperate with other services, or your service may be broadly based meaning that you wish to use more than one subject classification or keyword scheme. In this context, you will need to reconcile different schemes, or map one scheme to another, in the same way as you may map metadata schemes (see Chapter 21) to allow the exchange of records between services. In the realm of subject classification, this is done by directly mapping terms between schemes, or by developing thesauri to reconcile the use of different terms. Standards exist for the construction of monolingual thesauri (National Information Standards Organization, 1993). However, if you have chosen to use established subject classification and keyword schemes, then the task of mapping them will be much easier than if you have chosen to create your own schemes.

Another key aspect of the subject classification process is your indexing policy and how this will interact with user searches and navigation of your resource. You will need to decide what level of indexing of resources will be undertaken and how this will be offered to the user. You may opt to index everything on your resource to produce a text base of everything, so that users do not miss out on a single mention of a topic on your site. However, this can overwhelm users if your resource is large, and it can also produce false results. For example, a user looking for the social consequences of gambling will not want to retrieve a rulebook for different forms of gambling if both items are held by your resource and brought to them by a simple text-base search for 'gambling'. A change in your indexing and presentation policy can aid your users. For example, you can choose to index the titles and keywords of resources to form the database that a user will search. However, many users are as likely to want to browse your resource as they are to use a form and search it (Nielsen, 1997). After all, Google may offer a very simple and effective search mechanism via an online form, but it also includes a directory service of resources classified by subjects. Here, your subject classification or keyword scheme can really come into its own. The natural divisions you have used in your subject schemes can form the basis of a navigable structure for your website. Thus a resource covering the whole of the social sciences may have a major division dealing with economics and subdivisions detailing taxation, investment, corporate finance and so on. Your choice of subject classification is effectively reused to provide a logical, intuitive and navigable site structure which your users will be readily able to comprehend.

Resource issues and auto-classification

Whatever way of offering subject access to your resources you choose, it is very important to bear in mind that it will require large amounts of staff time and expertise. You may not be a practitioner in the field within which your information service operates; however, in order to be able to classify materials within it you will need to develop your expertise to a high level. The act of classifying materials is also time consuming, and while it may be broadly incorporated within the overall act of cataloguing materials for your service by adding appropriate metadata, getting it right will take time but will reap benefits for your users. While it may be tempting to let your users assign subjects and keywords, such uncontrolled vocabularies are likely to be hijacked by particular interest groups, which will produce unrepresentative, inconsistent and unusable data for your broader organisation.

> **Core Knowledge**
> Subject classification can be time-consuming and expensive, but the benefits are substantial.

One potential way of offering subject access to your materials without expending large amounts of staff time and effort is in the developing area of automatic concept generation. If your resources contain large amounts of text, this approach may be particularly useful, allowing them to be indexed and allocated to subjects. Complex mathematical theories are employed in such products, which have been developed for enterprise-level categorisation of documents for corporate intranets or suggesting other pages on related topics within news driven websites. As the algorithms used by such technologies are highly complex and developed as a consequence of much research, they are usually only available from companies specialising in this field, and often at a high cost. This approach is particularly useful in terms of providing related links and user recommendations, similar to the idea on *Amazon* of showing that users who bought item A also bought items B, C and D. However, it should be borne in mind that, as items are added to your resource in this system, the whole thing will be re-indexed and some items may well change their place within the concept map to reflect the evolving nature of your resource. This is good in terms of keeping the automatically generated concept tree up to date as a reflection of the collection as a whole (and is useful for Sandeep looking for information on SARS, for example). However, it may lead to some user confusion as resources move within the structure.

The overall goal of being able to use machine intelligence and semantic learning to automate out of existence human intervention in cataloguing and classifying resources is still some way off. Hopefully, it is now clear that there are plenty of tools out there to help make this process as painless as possible for you and to bring many benefits to your users.

Further reading

Bowker, G.C. and Leigh Star, S. (1999) *Sorting Things Out: Classification and Its Consequences*. Cambridge, MA: MIT Press.

Delphi Group (2002) *Taxonomy and Content Classification*. Available at: *http://www.delphigroup.com/coverage/taxonomy.htm*.

Ferguson, B. (1998) *Subject Analysis*. Englewood, CO: Libraries Unlimited.

21

Metadata

Debra Hiom

Of course, subject classification, as covered in the previous chapter, is a form of metadata (even when done automatically). While subject classification has been singled out for special attention, there are generic metadata issues that are assuming ever greater importance for information professionals.

What is metadata?

> Metadata is sometimes defined literally as 'data about data', but the term is normally understood to mean structured data about resources that can be used to help support a wide range of operations. These might include, for example, resource description and discovery, the management of information resources and their long-term preservation. (Day, 2001)

This quote neatly encapsulates both what is meant by metadata and its role in the information process. Metadata has also been referred to as 'a fancy name for an inferior form of cataloguing' (Gorman, 2000), and although this is rather an unfair assessment it does highlight the fact that the creation of metadata is very much in the realm of the information professional's role.

Why is it important?

If you are developing digital information resources, the creation and management of metadata can be an essential part of streamlining your internal and external practices. The growth of importance in metadata is linked to the growth of digital information, although it's important to note that metadata is not only used to describe electronic information resources. However, many forms of information now exist only in electronic form and metadata provides an effective tool for online services to manage their information and allow end-users to find and access this information. If the Web is ever to appear more structured and rigorous, as Olaf suggests it should (Chapter 7), then metadata is probably the key. It is also likely to be the basis for much repurposing and syndication of information, as Jeremy mentions (Chapter 6).

What is it used for?

One of the primary functions of metadata is to describe information objects. The descriptive metadata is usually a textual record but the actual objects that it is describing can be anything from text, images and sound recordings to streaming video and so on. This metadata can either be stored separately or embedded in the actual object that is being described. These descriptions can then be used to allow end-users of your service to find information through searching or browsing.

However, metadata also has a number of other functions such as rights management, version control and so on. Table 21.1 outlines the different types of metadata and their functions.

Choosing a metadata scheme

Choosing a format from the variety of existing metadata schemes will depend upon various factors, including availability of time, staff and the needs of your users. There are a number of specialist metadata schemes that have been created to deal with the particular needs of a subject or domain. For example, the *Data Documentation Initiative* (DDI) is a standard for describing social science datasets in data archives and the *Encoded Archival*

Table 21.2 Types of metadata

Type	Definition	Examples
Administrative	Metadata used in managing and administering information	■ Acquisition information ■ Rights and reproduction tracking ■ Documentation of legal access requirements ■ Location information ■ Selection criteria for digitisation ■ Version control and differentiation between similar information objects ■ Audit trails created by record-keeping systems
Descriptive	Metadata used to describe or identify information resources	■ Cataloguing records ■ Finding aids ■ Specialised indexes ■ Hyperlinked relationships between resources ■ Annotations by users ■ Metadata for record-keeping systems generated by records creators
Preservation	Metadata related to the preservation management of information resources	■ Documentation of physical condition of resources ■ Documentation of actions taken to preserve physical and digital versions of resources, for example data refreshing and migration
Technical	Metadata related to how a system functions or metadata behave	■ Hardware and software documentation ■ Digitisation information, for example formats, compression ratios, scaling routines ■ Tracking of system response times ■ Authentication and security data, for example encryption keys, passwords
Use	Metadata related to the level and type of use of information resources	■ Exhibit records ■ Use and user tracking ■ Content reuse and multi-versioning information

Source: Taken from Gilliland-Swetland (2000).

Description (EAD) is a standard for describing archival finding aids such as inventories, registers and indexes that are created by the archives, libraries and museum sector. The IEEE (*Institute of Electrical and Electronics Engineers*) has developed a standard specifically for describing educational learning and teaching materials. This has recently been adapted for use in a UK educational context and is called the *UK LOM Core*. These specialist schemes are valuable for their particular communities but are generally quite complicated and expensive to create and maintain.

Dublin Core

A more simple metadata scheme is the *Dublin Core*. The Dublin Core Metadata Initiative started out as a collaborative initiative between the academic, library, computing and publishing communities in 1995. The Dublin Core Metadata Element Set consists of 15 elements, designed for describing web-based resources across any subject or domain area, none of which are mandatory and any element can be repeated:

- *Subject*: the topic addressed by the work.
- *Title*: the name of the object.
- *Author*: the person(s) primarily responsible for the intellectual content of the object.
- *Publisher*: the agent or agency responsible for making the object available.
- *OtherAgent*: the person(s), such as editors and transcribers, who have made other significant intellectual contributions to the work.
- *Date*: the date of publication.
- *ObjectType*: the genre of the object, such as novel, poem or dictionary.
- *Form*: the physical manifestation of the object, such as Postscript file or Windows executable file.
- *Identifier*: string or number used to uniquely identify the object.
- *Relation*: relationship to other objects.

- *Source*: objects, either print or electronic, from which this object is derived, if applicable.
- *Language*: language of the intellectual content.
- *Coverage*: the spatial locations and temporal duration characteristic of the object.

As the name suggests the *Dublin Core* was an attempt to define the most basic set of elements needed to describe a web resource. In reality many of these elements are enriched by the use of qualifiers to refine a particular element. For example, the subject field might be extended by a qualifier that describes the use of a particular classification scheme such as the *Library of Congress Classification* (LOC) scheme or the *Dewey Decimal Classification* (DDC) scheme to describe the topic of the resource (see Chapter 20).

Issues of managing metadata

Granularity

This is the question of the level at which metadata is created, that is whether you choose to describe a single object or set of objects. For example, if you are providing an electronic journal through your online service, you may choose to create a record of each article or simply of each edition of the journal. Metadata creation is an expensive business and the lower the level of granularity you choose the more expensive it will become. These decisions should be informed by a good awareness of the needs and information-seeking behaviour of your users.

Encoding metadata

Metadata can be stored and expressed in a number of formats including text, HTML and XML. Text or HTML may be easier to understand and create but in the long run it may be more practical to use *XML* (*eXtensible Markup Language*). This is a standard developed specifically for use within large-scale electronic publishing environments. It provides a way of structuring and storing and exchanging information which can be defined by a DTD (document type definition). Unlike HTML, it carries no information on how to present the information. The XML standard is a project of the *W3C* (*World Wide Web Consortium*) and you can find details of the specification and some useful online tutorials on its website.

Storing metadata

As mentioned previously, metadata can be stored in the resource itself and there are some simple tools that make the creation of *Dublin Core* metadata within HTML encoded pages fairly easy. For example, *DC.dot* is a free tool that extracts metadata information from an HTML document and formats it so that it can be edited then cut and pasted back into the HTML header of the original document. Alternatively the metadata can be stored separately, typically in a searchable database. This has a number of advantages for sharing and exposing metadata in different environments but it does require careful linking of the metadata and the object it is describing.

Metadata conversion

One of the advantages of using well-defined and structured metadata formats is that this allows conversion into other formats when necessary. Format conversion is facilitated by the creation of crosswalks (or mapping tables) between metadata formats. Crosswalks can be used as the basis for the production of a specific conversion program or for the production of search systems that would permit the interrogation of heterogeneous metadata formats. A number of metadata format crosswalks have been published. One of the earliest DC-based crosswalks mapped *Dublin Core* to *USMARC*, and other crosswalks exist for other formats. A collection of metadata mappings is maintained on the *UKOLN* website.

Summary

Choosing a metadata format is an important decision that needs to be made when setting up your online information service. It is vital that the format is able to work with the software that forms the basis of the service and it should also contain all elements (including administrative metadata) that have been identified as appropriate for the users of your service. It is possible that ongoing changes in technologies may require periodic conversion of the database into new formats; this process will require the production of metadata crosswalks and/or format conversion programs.

Further reading

Brand, A. and Daly, F. (2003) *Metadata Demystified: A Guide for Publishers*. Hanover, PA: Sheridan Press/Bethesda, MD: NISO Press.

Heery, R., Powell, A. and Day, M. (1997) *Metadata*. London: Library Information Technology Centre.

Metadata Glossary: *http://www.ukoln.ac.uk/metadata/glossary/*.

22

Technology

Ale Fernandez and Claire Lumber

Introduction

This brief chapter about technology does not aim to be comprehensive or even, given the format in which it is published, up to date! However, you would certainly be surprised to find a book about online information systems lacking a chapter on technology. In a sense, this chapter is merely an overview and context for the more interesting possibilities outlined by Paul Shabajee in Chapter 24, but it also serves as a record of where we are now, in 2004, in relation to a few of the main technologies involved in online information services. It focuses on software, excluding desktop or office packages. It is intended as an overview of some of the important issues and options that are relevant to online information services, of which a manager of such a service should at least be aware. In writing this chapter, we have imagined that the online information service being produced is broadly a database-driven web resource, and thus that the key elements needed include content management or database systems, programming and scripting languages, and web technologies.

Basic choice: open source or proprietary?

In the software world, there is one overriding division, which is between those who use *Open Source* software and those who buy and use proprietary software. Open source software is developed by anyone with an interest in doing so, providing they make their developments available to the community (hence 'open source'). This unlikely sounding principle has led to a development effort of almost unimaginable size and sophistication, driven by the needs of those who build systems. Perhaps the best-known product of this effort is *Linux*, the Unix-based operating system that underlies most of the servers on the Web today. However, there is much more to open source than Linux. The benefits of taking the open source road are that you can draw on the collective effort of thousands of developers and that you are not locked into a proprietary solution with its regular and expensive upgrades. The drawbacks of open source include that software generally comes 'as seen', with documentation (perhaps) but few guarantees and sometimes not much backup, so that you need to have a technical developer who is comfortable with this. The assumption for the rest of this chapter, though, is that the open source route is both practically and philosophically more in keeping with the traditions and needs of the information profession. The focus, therefore, is mainly on open source options.

Programming and scripting languages

There is a wide variety of programming and scripting languages, and this section considers the headline strengths and weaknesses of some of them. The difference between programming and scripting is that the former is more concerned with calculations and file transformations, whereas the latter is more concerned with formatting, interactivity (for example, on the Web) and related manipulations. Of course, this is not a watertight distinction. In practice, it is unlikely that an online information service will have the luxury of choosing which language to use, since you will be dependent on both what expertise is available and what legacy and related systems are in place. The following are four of the more popular languages.

Perl (Practical Extraction and Report Language)

The catchphrase of *Perl* is that there is always more than one way to achieve anything. That is, given any task, *Perl* will offer a variety of candidate solutions. The drawback to this is that, unless your technical developer is an excellent programmer, the solution developed is unlikely to be absolutely optimal and may be hard to maintain unless very well documented. The advantage is that *Perl* is an amazingly flexible language. It is also one of the languages in which much open source software is written. It is especially good at text and data manipulation, moving data from databases to spreadsheets, file manipulation and so on. It can be object-oriented, if it is used in that way (but it needn't be). It can result in very fast operation, especially in tasks such as searching for string data within internal memory.

PHP (PHP Hypertext Preprocessor)

PHP is a language for web-based content presentation and has taken over from *Perl* as the most popular scripting language with which to action web forms. It is very easy to use and has good reference material available on the Web. However, there are question marks over its scalability, and it may tempt the unwary to mix functionality and presentation, given its use of both specialised PHP tags and HTML tags.

Python

Python is an easy-to-use object-oriented scripting language, similar in capability to *Perl* (though perhaps not as flexible) and *Java*. Its main use is as a 'glue' to enable other software modules (for example, those written in C variants) to work effectively together. Being stricter than *Perl*, it can result in code that is easier to maintain and understand, especially given its highly modular character. *Python* is rarely used on its own for web development, but more usually is used to add functionality within, for example, a *ZOPE* environment (see below).

Java

Java (developed by *Sun Microsystems*) is an object-oriented language that can result in high performance and speed (at the cost of higher memory requirements than some other languages). It has an open source version that works in a *Linux* environment. Compared with *Perl*, however, it may have inferior string handling, which is relevant when processing data from, say, a database or XML source.

As well as programming languages, there are also whole structured environments in which software can be developed and operated. While the following are by no means equivalent, they do exist at this higher level relative to the languages discussed above.

.Net

This is Microsoft's framework environment. You might think of it as an environment that bundles software modules together in a way that ensures they interoperate well. The modules can be written in C variants or *Perl* or *Java*, but within *.Net* they should work well together. There is a new open source version, called *Mono*.

ZOPE

The Z Object Publishing Environment is written in C and *Python*, and can be extended using *Python*. It has its own web development system, supports connections to databases such as *MySQL*, *PostgreSQL* and *Oracle* (see below), and can run using its own web server *Apache* (open source) or Microsoft's *IIS*. It now also has a dedicated content management system, '*Plone*'. It is popular and well supported, although it does have heavy demands on both processor and memory, which make it unwieldy for larger sites. It perhaps requires less technical expertise than *Perl* or the other programming languages, as (for example) web applications can be developed using a web browser and SQL statements can be used directly.

Databases and indexing

This is perhaps where the proprietary/open source distinction is sharpest, with (for example) *Oracle* and Microsoft's *SQL Server* on the one hand and *PostgreSQL* and *MySQL* on the other. Unless your institution has a site licence for the former, then they may not be options (especially *Oracle*, which is an industrial-strength database). Microsoft Access is, of course, a popular desktop database often used to drive websites, but it can suffer serious performance problems when several people use it simultaneously. *MySQL* is a small open source database, which can be very fast, but (certainly until recently) lacks many of the features of high-end databases. In particular, it is not fully transactional (that is, its operation is not based on transactions), which can lead to all kinds of problems and limitations, even if some of these can be worked around. *PostgreSQL* is closer to *Oracle,* though still open source. It has much greater functionality than *MySQL*, and is more scalable and probably more secure. It is, however, less easy to use (though developers used to commercial databases such as *Oracle* would find it familiar). Neither *MySQL* nor *PostgreSQL* come complete with the kind of end-user interface that Access users will be used to, although such tools can be added over the Web.

Indexing renders the database contents in a form suitable for searching or browsing. While many databases (for example, *Oracle*) include this functionality (*Oracle* indeed has its own sophisticated search tool), there can be reasons for using dedicated indexing tools. Indexes built by such tools as *Zebra* and *Cheshire*, for example, can support very fast searching, although without the relational functionality offered directly by database searches.

If databases and program code build the back-end of your resource, then the front-end is almost certain to run over a web interface (although this may be dynamically generated using the tools described above).

The Web

You will certainly be familiar with the old de facto web standard, HTML. This is the hypertext mark-up language, a language designed to support the presentation of hypertext in a networked environment. However, it is important to note that HTML is just that, a formatting or presentation mark-up, and does not describe the content of the page. For this, you need to use the new de facto web standard, XML. This is discussed in Chapter 24, along with the newer web developments such as personalisation and the Semantic Web. However, this chapter would not be complete (even within its radically incomplete ambitions) without at least a mention of the current buzzword, 'portals'.

Portals

Portals can mean almost anything to anyone, but one four-point checklist for a portal is as follows:

1. *Personalisation*. This is discussed further in Chapter 24 but basically involves the ability for the user to configure both the appearance and the available content to suit his or her needs. This can be achieved via the user explicitly stating their interests or identifying with a group whose interests can be inferred (for example, 'undergraduate student'), or by tracking user behaviour and inferring preferences from this data (this can be memory-hungry on large or popular sites).
2. *Cross-searching*. Searching across several sources is a key element in a portal, and can be achieved in a variety of ways, depending on the sources to be searched. Within an academic or library environment, the *Z39.50* standard (SRW within a 'Web Services' environment) allows databases and online catalogues to be cross-searched, and the Open Archives Initiative Protocol for Metadata Harvesting (*OAI-PMH*) standard promises an alternative method to roughly the same end. For content that is not hidden behind databases conventional web spiders or robots can be used to build local indexes of remote sources.

3. *Single-point authentication.* Some of the resources to be cross-searched may require authentication (confirming the user's identify) and authorisation (checking their privileges with this particular resource). Ideally, this is handled by the portal 'behind the scenes', with the user entering at most one username and password. Within the academic community, *Athens* is a key resource supporting authentication and authorisation.
4. *Embedded services.* Although portals can aim to be the 'one-stop shop' for a particular audience, it is often more effective to work with the grain of user behaviour and embed the portal functionality in websites or services that they already use. While this raises issues of branding and the provenance of the information made available in this way, these are surmountable with some effort and goodwill (see, for example, Learning and Teaching Portal Team, 2003).

One example of work toward these goals in the UK is the JISC *Subject Portals Project.*

System administration and hosting

These are issues that you should not have to think about, although you will need to confirm that they are being dealt with by someone! In particular, if these functions are contracted out, then you will need to take great care to ensure both that you have enforceable service level agreements and that you do not end up with a piecemeal IT structure.

Further reading

Relevant books from the O'Reilly series: *http://www.oreilly.com/.*

Part 3
The information issues

The final three chapters round off the book by looking a little more broadly at the information profession and, in particular, at the contexts in which we work. Although the chapters refer to 'social' and 'technological' contexts, in fact these labels may mask very similar developments. The final chapter draws from the whole book in offering one view of how the information professional might productively reflect on his or her role.

23

Social horizons

Neil Jacobs

Introduction

Both the case studies and the subsequent chapters have shown how such issues as currency, authority and information literacy are central to running information services. We have seen how users come to online services with increasing constraints, especially with respect to time, and rising expectations, both in terms of what is accessible and how quickly it can be delivered. We have also seen how the traditional skills of the information professional (selection, classification and so on) can be effectively deployed in these conditions. However, what about the wider context? Reflective practitioners aim to anticipate demands and be in a position to meet them, and this means that information professionals need to scan horizons – technical, organisational and social.

In this final part of the book, we look at some of the broad trends and theories in society, organisations and technology to identify how these will be played out in online information services. While the earlier parts of the book have been focused on the relationship between the user and the service, this section is more concerned with the relationship between both of these and the outside world. It is a commonplace now to talk of the 'information society' and the 'knowledge economy', to think about services tailored to people's needs rather than mass production, and to respond by saying that a key theme in how people, organisations and societies deal with all of this is 'learning'. But where do these ideas come from, and what do they mean for professionals and practitioners on the ground? This part firstly takes a brief tour through some of the most common theories, and then looks in more detail at the specific technologies that are important in the information society. The final chapter considers how all this relates to running an online information service.

Globalisation

Manuel Castells is certainly one of the key theorists of globalisation, and of what he calls the 'network society' (Castells, 2000). What he means by this is that 'the global economy is based on the ability of the core activities – meaning money, capital markets, production systems, management systems, information – to work as a unit in real time on a planetary scale' (Castells and Kreisler, 2001). It is as well to be clear about this idea, since much follows from it. Castells is not saying that trade is international (it has been for millennia), or that networks are important (again, this is not new), but that we live in a society

> where the key social structures and activities are organized around electronically processed information networks. So it's not just about networks or social networks, because social networks have been very old forms of social organization. It's about social networks which process and manage information and are using micro-electronic based technologies. (Castells and Kreisler, 2001)

Some people have argued that this theory places too much emphasis on the technology at the expense of people and social and economic factors. However, if we see the theory as a tool to help us think about broad trends that are otherwise difficult to capture, then it is certainly of some use.

Castells' view brings together, or is related to, a number of other concepts, such as the 'post-industrial society' and the 'mode of information'. The 'post-industrial society' idea was first coined by

American sociologist Daniel Bell some 30 years ago (Bell, 1974) to describe a trend he saw largely in rich, western countries where an increasing proportion of the workforce was not actually making things but was engaged in what might be called broadly the service sector. Clearly, online information services are a part of this sector although, since information services have been around since the Library at Alexandria, it is not clear that they form a part of any recent trend in terms of numbers of people employed. However, Bell goes further and emphasises that behind the demographic trend is a rise in the importance of codified, technical knowledge for the economy and society. Here is where the importance of online information services is key because, as in Castells's network society, the crucial success factor in the modern world is the effective deployment of reliable and relevant information.

Other thinkers have pointed to different consequences of this development. Mark Poster has described, among other things, a shift from the 'mode of production' to the 'mode of information', which closely parallels Bell's shift from industrial to post-industrial society (Poster, 1990). Poster was influenced by the great French thinker, Foucault. In terms of online information services, he drew from Foucault's redescription of Jeremy Bentham's 'panopticon', a prison where the inmates changed their behaviour because they were aware that they might be under surveillance at any moment without knowing it. Poster argued that the Internet and online databases offer the potential for a 'super-panopticon', where we cannot help but to leave traces and evidence of our activities that can be observed, recorded and combined later. This means that, in effect, there are digital versions of 'me' out there, which are made up of all the electronic traces I left when I visited websites and databases. Knowing this may make me change my behaviour, either because I want to influence what these digital versions look like, or because those who 'own' them (the database owners) can use them in their marketing and other activities.

We live, then, in a global village, where an increasing number of actors (governments, corporations, organisations, people) decide how to behave by reference to electronic sources of information, models and simulations. In the field of higher education, for example, more and more researchers are making their papers available online before they are published, discussing them in real time with peers across the world using electronic communications and revising them accordingly. This can also lead to new avenues of research being considered or existing proposals being rejected, changing both the shape of research and the processes that make it up. Of course, it can also lead to untested material being widely available. As Jack Meadows (1998) notes, 'with the mass media becoming increasingly concerned with information from electronic sources, such dubious material may be called to the attention of a much wider audience who are in no position to judge its acceptability.' But the consequences of a globalised, information society are much broader than this. The Oxford sociologist Steve Woolgar (2002) has noted that: 'Electronic technologies facilitate the rapid traffic in communication, the instantiation of activities and institutions at widespread locales, and the insinuation of standardized identities and imagery (especially brands) in multiple locations.' That is, communication, action and identity now have a completely different relationship with space and distance, just as Castells has argued.

However, some barriers may remain. For example, while only perhaps one in ten people in the world speak English as a native language, around 80 per cent of websites are in English. The *Global Reach* site has estimated that only around 36 per cent of people using the Internet are native English speakers, a proportion that has been falling consistently for several years. By contrast, the English language community dominates e-commerce, the dollar value of online transactions among the English-speaking nations being an order of magnitude, if not more, greater than that of any other language community. Largely, of course, this is due to the dominance of the United States. However, while English is becoming the unofficial second language of international communities (such as the EU), US brands and identities are encountering resistance, and global companies are having to tailor their goods and services to local conditions. We see here the signs of globalisation's twin – localisation.

Localisation

I quoted above from Steve Woolgar's introduction to the book *Virtual Society?* (2002). In this book, he outlines what he calls 'five rules of virtuality', or five maxims that seem to hold in contemporary society. One of these is 'the more global, the more local', which is to say the more electronic technologies seem to connect the whole world into a single virtual reality, the more local considerations in fact come to the fore. For example, the implementation of an intranet within an organisation will probably result in attempts to make explicit some of the tacit knowledge held by the people who work there about how things are done, who holds particular 'how-to' knowledge and so on. If it is to be successful, the intranet will need to reflect these local factors at least as clearly as it does the global logic of the default software, the organisational structure of the host or the international standards of professional practices such as accountancy. However, this overarching principle perhaps hides some of the ways in which the same trends that are reconfiguring the world at a global level are also working at the local level, changing the way local factors work at the same time as emphasising their importance.

One of the key concepts we can get from Castells is that of the 'informatisation of process'. What this unpleasant piece of jargon means is that an increasing proportion of the tasks that we do, both in the workplace and at home, are becoming infused with information processing. In some ways he is pointing to what the controversial social theorist Jean Baudrillard calls 'the code', or the ways in which real events are being displaced by online simulations. However, Castells is much more interested in how these online models and simulations affect the ways we live and work. For example, transnational corporations routinely monitor and act on processed, reliable, real-time information from around the world in order to make decisions about investment, resource deployment and so on. At the same time, a glut of potentially unreliable information is available to less privileged actors. At the local level, this means that there is an increasing level of uncertainty, because reliable information is restricted to powerful organisations, so that consequent decisions are therefore unpredictable by those outside who must rely on potentially unreliable information. This is just one aspect of what is termed the 'digital divide' (Warschauer, 2002), which describes how the growing importance of information is reflected in radically uneven access to it.

Informatisation in the workplace has gone alongside a move to what sociologists call 'post-fordist' production methods. While this move applies equally to the manufacturing and service sectors, it may be easier to describe it within a manufacturing context. Fordism refers to the high-volume, mass production model based on the assembly line. Post-fordism, or 'flexible specialisation', refers to a succeeding model where products (or services) are turned out in smaller quantities, fitted more to niche markets or needs. To achieve this level of specialisation, work processes need to use technical or expert knowledge, which may be from people (lawyers, economists, designers) or be embodied in machines (computer-controlled machine tools, decision support systems, online information systems). To the extent that the expertise comes from people, then this is Daniel Bell's vision of the post-industrial society. To the extent that it is embodied in machines, then this may relate to Castells's 'informatisation of process'.

So, how are these features of the modern workplace reflected in the ways in which people interact with information? One rather helpful metaphor that has gained some currency is that of the 'information ecology'. Just as a particular set of biological entities (plants, animals, the environment) exist in a balanced state where there is a web of dependencies, so we can think about people in the same way. Bonnie Nardi and Vicky O'Day (1999) have defined an information ecology as being a 'system of people, practices, values, and technologies in a particular local environment. In information ecologies, the spotlight is not on technology, but on human activities that are served by technology.' The role of the information service then becomes akin to that of a gardener, promoting the growth of good information practices, weeding out sources of misinformation and ensuring that people work in an information environment that supports them. Increasingly, this leads to perhaps the ultimate in localisation, that is personalisation.

Technology?

This chapter has had a strong theoretical slant to it in order to bring to the surface some of the key issues facing the social and organisational worlds. There are several ways to approach issues such as global interoperability, surveillance, standardisation and personalisation. In the next chapter Paul Shabajee discusses some of the technologies that are involved in these processes, especially as they relate to online information services. In the past, perhaps, professionals and managers of information services have been more consumers of technologies than participants in its development. Wider social forces and rapid technical developments now mean that those running online information services need to be more engaged in shaping the next generation of architectures. So far as infrastructure developments are concerned, a 'watching brief' may be all that is required. However, because they relate directly to the wider social contexts discussed in this chapter, user-oriented developments such as ontology creation, personalisation techniques and interface design are key areas where practitioners need to get involved.

24

Technological horizons

Paul Shabajee

Previous chapters have described what can be characterised as a co-evolution of technological and human (organisational, social and individual) systems. This chapter details and briefly explores some of the implications of newer and evolving technologies. It starts by looking at the wider context of ICT, before looking at new developments in a little detail, covering three areas of interest: hardware, information and knowledge, and the human interface.

Wider contexts of ICT

One consequence of the rapid development of technologies, and equally dramatic and co-evolutionary changes in behaviour, is that perceived time frames have shrunk. This is particularly true with respect to changes in information technology and service provision, such as the provision of mobile phone texting and related information services. These services range from weather reports to restaurant guides to 'tell me what this piece of music is called'. These have developed in only five years or so, since the widespread take-up of SMS (Short Message Service) messaging. The gap between 'bleeding edge' and 'old hat' technology is, in some cases, very short indeed. SMS is but one example of so-called 'disruptive technologies' (Christensen, 1997), which interfere with, sidestep and displace traditional ways of doing things. Those of us involved in information provision in an information economy can be expected to feel such disruption, and have to adapt to it, more than most.

Traditionally, it has been the case that information services have been focused on serving users in desk-based environments using static networked computers, and this is reflected in the previous chapters of this book. The implications of many of the current technologies, especially those related to mobility, are therefore likely to be dramatic for information service providers.

In that context, it is worth spending a little time taking a broader view of how new information technologies are being introduced and developing. 'Convergence' was a buzzword of the 1990s, and one that has become more than simply that. The reality is all around us. The much-predicted convergence of telecommunications, computers and computer networks, television and radio is all but complete (for example, in many home appliances and mobile devices), with technologies in single pieces of equipment or linked together by cable, infrared or short-range radio signals such as *Bluetooth*.

However, it has not stopped there. The advent, integration and rapid take-up of 'broadband' networking, mobile phone SMS texting services (Gupta, 2000), computer-based instant messaging (Bennett, 2003), digital cameras and global positioning system (GPS) devices, for example, have added new potentials to the original ideas of 'convergence'.

These, together with the secure connections to institutional, home or commercial computer networks across the public Internet enabled by Virtual Private Networks (VPN Consortium, 2003), secure e-commerce transactions and digital signatures and certificates, make it possible for 'mobile professionals' or the most casual of users to access even sensitive data and information services, almost anywhere at any time.

It is in this context, where networked technology is potentially ubiquitous, that newer and evolving information technologies need to be viewed. The word 'potentially' in the previous sentence is important; issues of the 'digital divide' are likely to be no less relevant in this context than they are today (Light, 2001). The 2003 edition of *How Much Information?* (Lyman and Varian, 2003) estimates that 'about 600 million people have access to the Internet, about 30% of them in North America'. This can be compared with an estimated population of the Earth of over six billion.

The remainder of this chapter provides a whistle-stop tour of some newer and evolving technologies and their implications. It is divided broadly into three parts, the first focused on hardware and infrastructure, the second on knowledge capture, representation, management, dissemination and integration, and the third on interfaces, customisation, personalisation, and users, both as individuals and as members of communities of interest or practice.

Hardware and infrastructure

In the previous section, we have briefly explored some aspects of the current technological contexts. This section looks a little further forward at a few of the most significant of the many relevant 'hardware platform' and infrastructure developments.

Storage

It is likely that current growth in the storage capacity of information devices of all kinds will continue. A fairly standard office desktop computer comes with 80 or more gigabytes of hard disk (one gigabyte = 10^9 bytes). There is no reason to believe that terabyte (one terabyte = 10^{12} bytes) personal local storage will not be very far away, for example on a PC or hard-disk based digital video recorder. At an institutional level, petabyte (one petabyte = 10^{15} bytes) storage systems are already used in research and large corporate systems, such as that of the *Council for the Central Laboratory of the Research Councils* in the UK. The development of grid and 'utility computing' (see below) means that this trend is likely to increase. This may mean that we reach a point where storage volume ceases to be an issue, although it is possible that, with increased capacity, applications will evolve that require greater and greater levels of storage. This has tended to be the case in the past.

There are many consequences and potentials of such massive storage, both positive and negative. It becomes essentially unnecessary to discard any information. For information services, this means that all information that they have ever held can be both securely archived and still available on a live system. It would be possible to track every editing and management event of every document or piece of data (of any type) at every stage of its life. An extreme example of this is from the USA, where the Pentagon's so-called 'LifeLog' project (Schachtman, 2003) is exploring whether it is possible to gather 'every conceivable element of a person's life, dump it all into a database, and spin the information into narrative threads that trace relationships, events and experiences'. While this may be a limited view of *a person's life*, it does illustrate the scale of the potential.

Grid, utility and adaptive computing

The basic idea behind grid and utility computing is that it is possible, using computer networking, to access computing power, software and services remotely. The UK government *Department of Trade and Industry e-Science and Grid* website explains grid computing as follows.

> The word 'Grid' is chosen by analogy with the electric power grid, which provides pervasive access to power and, like the computer and a small number of other advances, has had a dramatic impact on human capabilities and society. We believe that by providing pervasive, dependable, consistent and inexpensive access to advanced computational capabilities, databases, sensors and people, computational grids will have a similar transforming effect, allowing new classes of applications to emerge.

The impact of these technologies on information providers and their users might be expected to be dramatic. In practice, these systems aim to allow users to purchase or loan access to what is, in effect, a super-computer, customised to a particular type of problem, with any required software and hardware configuration.

It can be available almost instantly, for time periods of anything from seconds to the life of a project or organisation, and scalable to meet particular needs. Developments at present are rapid, and utility data centre and grid-based systems are common in research institutions. However, the technologies needed to provide the full range of services and applications are not yet in place, and significant research is still required to make these a reality.

In information service terms, this means that users could in principle run real-time analysis across whole sets of data corpuses, using bespoke statistical algorithms, data mining techniques or visualisation techniques. The volumes of data and rate of processing offered by such systems are orders of magnitude greater than using existing institutional facilities.

In the context of developments such as the Semantic Web (see below), these approaches bring the potential of previously unimaginable dynamic data integration and synthesis, analysis and processing.

Faster networks

The definition of broadband networking has changed dramatically over the last ten years. In 1996, 64 kbps (kilobits per second, ISDN connection) was considered broadband in the home market. Today it is nearer 1–2 Mbps (megabits per second, using ASDL or cable access). Such speed developments are likely to continue, largely due to the heavy commercial pressure to provide services such as video on demand. Within corporate and academic networks, speeds can be very much faster. SuperJanet, the UK academic network (*Janet*), has a core network running at speeds of 10 Gbps (gigabits per second or 1,000 Mbps). For comparison, a cable TV channel requires about 2–6 Mbps.

For information providers, increasing bandwidth means that users may have access to very large data files or rich multimedia data. These fast networks underlie the development of grid type technologies.

Ubiquitous, invisible, pervasive or wearable, 'always on' computing

The convergence and ubiquity described above is part of a trend toward more integrated and mobile computing. The terms ubiquitous, invisible, pervasive and wearable computing describe aspects of the trend towards computers simply becoming part of a synthetic real/virtual environment. They become effectively invisible, more ubiquitous than pen and paper. When the Internet and other networked connections are 'always on', there is no 'shall I log on and check my e-mail or look this up?' barrier. The connection is always live and the information always available.

Examples of this kind of computing are projects such as the *Mobile Bristol* research project, in which 'the vision of the test-bed is to provide a digital canvas over the city onto which rich situated digital experiences can be painted and new commercial ventures can be explored'.

Common characteristics of these developments are mobility and technology that provide users with services situated in their specific context, which might relate to their personal preferences, their business or their geographical location. For information providers, there are many opportunities and challenges based on customisation and personalisation, and these are discussed further below.

Knowledge capture, representation, management, dissemination and integration

The title of this section may appear too long. However, the reason that these issues are explored together is that they are all intimately interrelated. Since the development and widespread use of computer databases and their associated access interfaces (such as OPAC library and archive management systems), networked computer technology has provided an impressive set of advantages over traditional card- and paper-based information management systems. Indeed they have been so successful and widely adopted that it is easy to forget that many libraries still used card catalogues until the mid to late 1980s and beyond. These advantages include ease of data maintenance, sharing of data, increased quality control (for example, via access to national and international authority files), faceted/multidimensional querying and, more recently, the full-text searching of whole works and corpuses, access to rich multimedia, integrated communications (for example, between staff and users of a service) and basic levels of data integration via information portals.

All of these capabilities depend fundamentally for their effectiveness and their limitations on their underlying knowledge capture, representation and management technologies. However, these aspects of systems are often effectively invisible to users. Many of the associated (generally technical) issues and their implications are little known even to many staff involved in information provision. Some of these are explored in this section.

Volume and types of information

If we look at the capture of data at the trivial level of volume, the situation is stark. There are many estimates for various types of data, but Lyman and Varian (2003) estimate that the amount of new information stored on paper, film and magnetic and optical media has grown by 30 per cent for each year from 1999 to 2002. The sources of this growth are varied, although web-based data is probably of most relevance here. Lyman and Varian estimate, roughly, that there are some 92,000 terabytes of data accessible via the Web. By comparison, if digitised, the US Library of Congress print collection would total some 10 terabytes.

It is an open question how much of this growth is of interest to information workers. Indeed, the term 'information overload' (discussed in previous chapters) is largely caused by this growth. However, there are many specific examples that clearly are of relevance. These include very large national and international digitisation projects in the areas of cultural heritage, such as the

UK New Opportunities Fund Digitisation Programme, covering museums and cultural objects, historic documents, images, video and so on. It is not uncommon to hear of digital repositories with hundreds of thousands or even millions of objects.

E-learning resources are also a major area of growth. The majority of universities in the UK, for example, are developing electronic content management systems and managed or virtual learning environments. There are also some fundamentally new models of publishing that are having significant impacts, such as e-print archives and blogging. Academic e-print archives are repositories where researchers publish their papers prior to, or sometimes following, publication (Pinfield, Gardner and MacColl, 2002). In some academic areas, e-print archives are becoming a primary mode of publication, with many advantages, including very significantly reduced latency between experiment, writing and publication. Another example is blogging (*weblogging*), which is a simple means to publish personal or community information onto the web from any computer with a web connection (Blood, 2000). This was highlighted during the 2003 Iraq war, with the Baghdad Blogger (McCarthy, 2003) providing news from inside the country. Google recently purchased the company Blogger, which is the largest provider of blogging services in the world. Blogging, both individually and as a member of a wider community, is illustrative of a wider growth in what might be thought of as community-based knowledge creation, discussed further below.

The types of information are evolving too. For example, it is now common to find interactive online learning courses, 3D environments and objects, and e-commerce-based purchase of products and services of almost any kind in almost every sphere of the economy.

Finding and retrieving information

Clearly, the ability to locate resources is a prerequisite for the effective development of information services. This is reflected in the very large number of academic and commercial attempts to improve information retrieval across web-based data. Approaches that have been tried for textual data include complex textual analysis and concept extraction algorithms (such as those offered by *Adiuri* and *Autonomy*), and the uses of thesauri to map from query term to the appropriate indexing terms. In the case of multimedia data (for an overview, see the *TASI Searching for and Retrieving Digital Images* page), content-based image retrieval is a leading approach. It uses the characteristics of a still or moving image, such as the colour or textual patterns and shapes, to identify the content and link that to a query term.

Perhaps the oldest, and yet in web terms relatively under-developed, approach is the use of metadata and standardised vocabularies to describe and index all aspects of a piece of information, of any type (for current practice, see Chapters 20 and 21). These schemas provide definitions for what pieces of data are to be represented, and sets of rules about how the pieces of data are related and what values they can take. For example, a library 'accession_date' must be part of a set of data about a library item and must take the form dd:mm:yyyy. Within traditional libraries and archives, such standards are almost as old as libraries and archives themselves. There is now a significant growth in the number of metadata standards and schemas as it becomes clear that ever more areas of the wider 'information space' require clear metadata standards in order to locate and share information effectively.

Once a metadata schema and associated vocabularies are specified, it has traditionally been the case that human cataloguers and indexers carried out the skilled task of applying the standards. In the past, the complexities of the tasks have meant that computers could not perform them. However, there are many disadvantages to using humans. These include cost, time, the high degree of knowledge and skills and thus training required, and the relatively poor inter-indexer consistency achieved when using large taxonomies (Markey, 1984). There is much research into ways of replacing or assisting humans in these cataloguing and indexing tasks, including investigations of machine learning techniques such as neural networks and artificial immune system models (Greensmith and Cayzer, 2003), and knowledge representation technologies such as machine readable ontologies (see below). These approaches are possible because much of the content to be indexed is in digital format, a prerequisite for such systems!

Systems that automatically 'discover' categories within data and metadata are also being investigated. These use similar techniques to those of concept extraction for direct retrieval of documents or other resources, also employing statistical, probabilistic and machine learning technologies. Such approaches may make older static metadata standards redundant. If a system can adjust to the needs of a number of user groups dynamically, why impose static systems with limited foci? There are, of course, a number of good reasons to do so, such as consistency over time and ensuring interoperability. However, in principle, parallel systems cannot be developed and utilised as appropriate.

Improved storage and retrieval technologies are creating new possibilities and business models for information access. One dramatic example is the introduction in October 2003 of a service by Amazon in the USA called *Amazon Search Inside the Book*. They had digitised about 120,000 books and provided free text searching across that data and, in some cases, provided access to images of the underlying pages to those who registered with their credit card details. Such developments may well undermine traditional structures and models of use. Researchers may, for example, be well advised to use vast Amazon type commercial databases of the future to locate relevant books, and even potentially view the relevant pieces of text.

Joining information together

Potentially even more profound is the goal of many to develop the means to join disparate data from across the Web together by making web content more 'machine readable' or machine processible. The potential for such joining, integration and so inter-operation is quite simply unimaginable to us today. A simple example, away from traditional information service provision, illustrates the level of integration envisaged and some of the implications. At present, it is possible to pre-book all aspects of almost any type of holiday online, from the taxi from home to the half-day excursion from the hotel to the car hire. However, at present a human is required to locate and collate the vast majority of such data. The goal of web-scale integration is that such diverse data as travel details, hotel information, government travel guidance, travel products and services and so on can all be located and integrated *automatically* by computer programs widely called 'agents', providing users with a range of available options based on their pre-defined preferences.

As discussed in Chapter 23, HTML is designed to instruct a computer how to display data, not what the data itself means or is about. The HTML tags around, say, a person's name and address would not allow any computer program to make use of the fact that that piece of text was about a person or an address. This is the primary reason that designing web search engines is difficult.

XML (eXtensible Mark-up Language) is now commonly used in web-based information systems and was developed, in part, to begin to overcome the limitations of HTML. Using XML and associated XML vocabularies or *schema*, it is possible to build web-based content and associated computer programs that can take the data and process it, to extract and make use of it. This is because programs can be designed to 'understand' the particular schema. This makes the sharing of data across the Web much simpler and more standardised than using bespoke databases with fixed structures. XML also has a number of advantages over a traditional relational database in the way that data can be represented. It is for these reasons that XML forms the basis of many e-commerce and other data-sharing applications.

However, in order for a computer program to be able to process XML data, it must be designed to make use of the appropriate schema. A 'date' in one document (and hence one schema) may represent the same type of data as a 'date' in another, but because the data is structured differently, a computer program designed only for one cannot make use of the other without some, often significant, reprogramming. Adding new types of data to an XML data model is also problematic. This is because both the schema and therefore any computer programs that use it are very likely to require editing in order to work safely with the new schema and to make use of the new data. XML is, therefore, not sufficient on its own.

The *W3C* (World Wide Web Consortium, the organisation that defines technical standards such as HTML and XML for the Web) has developed a set of technologies and standards together called the Semantic Web (see the *W3C Semantic Web* page). In basic terms, Semantic Web technologies and standards allow for the generation of web-based information that machines can process more automatically, because the structure of the data is not so tightly defined as in the case of XML and it is designed with the implicit knowledge that new types of data are likely to be added. The language of the Semantic Web is called RDF (Resource Description Framework). RDF is capable of representing 'semantic' relationships between data, metadata elements and terms. Fundamental is the allocation of unique identifiers (URI – Uniform Resource Identifiers) for objects, concepts and the relationships between them. When coupled with machine-readable ontologies (see below), this allows systems to be sure that they are talking about the same things using the same concepts. Hence the name: 'Semantic Web'.

Semantic Web data and ontologies can be combined with simple inferencing to allow users to conduct queries that were previously not possible. For example, if an ontology encodes that a particular ceramicist lived during a particular period in time then, using simple inferencing, a retrieval system can infer that all items made by that ceramicist are of that period and thus return items related to them from queries related to those dates. With more advanced machine learning approaches (see, for example, Negnevitsky, 2002) computer-based agents may be able to conduct much more powerful, knowledge-based activities.

Capturing knowledge?

Another necessary layer of the Semantic Web is machine-readable 'knowledge' about a topic. A thesaurus is a basic example of this;

it allows a user to type in one keyword and the computer maps that term to an indexing term. However, even simple information queries require 'deeper' knowledge. For example, a user of a database might what to find all images of animals that fly. However, unless the database system 'knows' which animals fly, such a query would fail. No human would or could ever index every bird image with 'flight' and every other possible behaviour of every species in the image. This knowledge needs to be encoded in a machine-readable format. The Semantic Web draws on long-standing work developing 'machine readable ontologies' (see the *W3C OWL Web Ontology Language Overview*) that can codify such knowledge and make it available to, for example, search engines to 'understand' the query of a user.

However, the creation of ontologies is complex and problematic. Encoding human knowledge that is often incomplete, disputed, conditional and changing is currently beyond most (possibly all) computer-based approaches. Where knowledge is encoded in an ontology, the implications of accepting (using) the ontology are also academically and philosophically problematic. For example, it is easy and, in most relevant contexts, generally useful to encode the 'fact' that Shakespeare is the author of all of 'Shakespeare's works'. However, at an academic level this is a controversial statement. Encoded deep within a machine-readable ontology, the 'fact' becomes effectively invisible.

These issues notwithstanding, Semantic Web technologies can, in principle, enable automatic and semi-automatic web-scale integration of data, and thus reach the goal of automatically joining up data, be it for grid-type computing or for booking holidays.

Web services

'Web services' is another element of joining distributed information and services together on the Web. The term 'services' can be misleading; as used at present, it refers to services for computers *not* people. It is basically a means for one computer (on the Web) to ask another computer to run a program and return it the results. It is another area of rapid standards development that can be monitored on the *W3C Web Services Activity* page.

The services can be almost anything. The requesting computer may send some data, such as details of a product, a person's name or a whole collection of multimedia. The processing computer can (in principle) return almost anything in response, such as a product price or availability or a piece of video transcoded into a new format. At present, dominant applications are in the area of e-commerce. However, there are rapidly evolving services in the education and libraries domain as well, for example terminology services, proposed as part of the HILT project (Heery, 2003).

As web services evolve and become more standardised, it is likely that many more processes (and associated data) will become distributed using services spread across the Web, with the potential for significant gains in interoperability and reductions in the duplication of effort and costs.

Users, interfaces, personalisation, communities

All the developments outlined above lead to wide-ranging issues and potentials both for users as individuals and as members of groups and communities, and for information professionals who provide access for those users via user interfaces on various types of device.

However, there is no archetypal information user. There is not even a stable, statistically average information user or any other static model of a 'user', however complex that model may be. This is simply because, as noted at the start of this chapter, as systems evolve so do users – in their expertise, awareness and, perhaps most strikingly, in their expectations. While some elements might be thought of as aspects of fashion (for example, some aspects of interface design), others are longer term. These latter include expectations of response times, the quality of metadata and the interlinking and interoperation of data.

An interesting perception is that recent generations can be thought of as 'digital natives', whereas older generations are 'digital immigrants' (Prensky, 2001). The argument is that the younger generation is embedded within an electronically oriented culture. They are, for example, more capable of multitasking and dynamically integrating different sources of information from multiple electronic sources. The phrase 'continuous partial attention', coined by Linda Stone (quoted in Friedman 2001), seems to describe our psychological state well in such situations. The state of affairs in schools is an interesting illustration. Prensky illustrates this in one student who noted resentfully that he had to 'power down' as he entered school. That is, he had to turn off his electronic and communications devices, devices that form significant parts of the basic fabric of the rest of his life. As designers and developers of information services, we need to be aware that there is a clear and present risk that we might be designing systems for 'digital immigrants' by 'digital immigrants', and all but ignoring the needs and expectations of 'digital natives'.

User interfaces are critical elements of any information service. The most amazing state-of-the-art knowledge integration and management system is of little value if users cannot navigate and locate the information that they require. The design of ergonomic (user-friendly) interfaces is thus a holy grail for any information provider. As the complexity and integration of information grow, the challenge to interface designers can become overwhelming. For example, at the most basic level, a computer monitor displays two-dimensional representations of information that may have very many dimensions or facets. Geographic information, historical information, scientific models, subject headings, authors, formats and sources may all fall into this category. Mapping these many-dimensional data onto a two-dimensional screen in a way that humans (especially untrained humans) can 'take it in' is massively problematic.

There are many creative examples of recent attempts to help users access complex and multifaceted information using traditional screen-based interfaces. These range from the e-commerce examples of *Amazon* to portal-type interfaces such as those within the *JISC Information Environment* and visualisation experiments by organisations such as the Smithsonian, for example the *HistoryWired* and *RevealingThings* project interfaces. Three-dimensional virtual reality modelling is already commonly used for museum objects, architectural and archaeological modelling and, of course, computer game environments.

Traditionally, interfaces have been custom designed. However, such approaches are costly and simply impractical where data and data types are dynamic (for example, a user might want to visualise a spreadsheet of contacts data via a map interface or an organisational chart or using many other 'views'). The development of flexible interfaces capable of such dynamic change, which might be called 'data aware', is underway. The key challenge is to model the data in a way that allows the software to 'know' how particular types of data can be represented or joined and dynamically reconfigured into particular visualisations. Data and metadata standards are critical components in such developments. Research environments such as *Haystack* are exploring these possibilities.

The synthetic environment created when virtual and real spaces are joined means that interfaces can be far more diverse than a two-dimensional screen. Data gloves and other 'immersive interfaces' provide yet more ways to interact with and visualise information. However, perhaps even more significant in practice is the development of services and associated interfaces that integrate data from real and virtual sources, to provide users with contextual information. These are applications that are, for example, aware of their location or task, and are under development as an aspect of ubiquitous computing (see the section on hardware and infrastructure, above).

These last examples are closely related to the customisation and personalisation of information services. Information portals dating from early commercial developments such as MyYahoo! have offered relatively sophisticated customisation. While the previous paragraphs have discussed technologies that enable users to customise their interfaces and integrate information, just as important is the ability of services to monitor and automatically adapt to the user. This kind of approach is illustrated most strongly in commercial services such as *Amazon*, which can provide various kinds of 'automatic' customisation. This personalisation includes the ability to suggest related titles based on previous choices and a vast statistical database of the navigation and purchasing choices of millions of other users. It provides the basis of 'if you like this, you may be interested in...' type of feedback, and it is also used to customise advertising. This kind of monitoring of user activity is a powerful illustration of the fact that users are not, and cannot be, isolated when using information systems. It is likely that we are only just beginning to explore the implications of this kind of adaptation.

It is sometimes hard to remember that the concept of networked 'virtual communities' is not yet mature. Our understanding of these communities, their needs and behaviours is a critical issue in developing effective information services. Understanding the technologies and their evolving uses, which are often very different from those originally intended, is a critical element in knowing our users. At present one very strong theme is 'communities of users' (of a piece of software, system or website), sharing information outside *traditional* channels. Blogging, peer-to-peer file sharing and instant messaging are well known examples of this. Collaborative information resources such as *Wikipedia* and *H2G2* are another significant area.

A further dramatic example of 'communities' working together is the rise of open source software development (see Chapter 22) in which individuals and, in many cases, commercial companies work together to develop software tools and applications for 'the community' (everyone) that are free to use and develop. Hand in hand with such development comes different types of intellectual property arrangements, such as *Copyleft* and *Creative Commons*, which reflect what is already a significant change in attitudes among many towards information in general.

In conclusion

This chapter has aimed to give just a glimpse of a variety of technologies and issues related to them that are likely to have significant impacts on those of us providing information services. I am sure that many readers could add to the examples given above. The picture that is painted is one in which the role of information providers is changing, co-evolving with technologies and users.

At present this co-evolution is taking place at a blindingly rapid pace which can feel daunting. It can also mean that there is little time for reflection about the need for, or implications of, the introduction of new technologies. A poignant quote that is often cited in this context dates from 1854 when Henry David Thoreau noted that: 'Our inventions are wont to be pretty toys, which distract our attention from serious things. They are but improved means to an unimproved end, an end which it was already but too easy to arrive at' (Thoreau, 1854).

As providers of information services it will often fall to us to make judgements about the potential value of new and potentially disruptive technologies. Is this thing just a pretty toy? What 'end' is it a means to? Is it a solution we have been seeking for our problems or a solution seeking problems? Or is it highlighting a whole new kind of problem? Second-guessing the future is possibly the most difficult and nerve-wracking side of innovation.

As a sector, perhaps we need to take a more active part in helping to answer these and many other questions much earlier in the technological development cycle. We could, and perhaps should, become more involved in the inception and design of technologies, rather than be all too often passive consumers of them.

25

From need to service: the changing role of the information professional

Lesly Huxley and Neil Jacobs

Introduction

The last two chapters have scanned both the social and technological horizons. These are, perhaps, the widest contexts for both users of information services and the information professionals who provide them. The earlier parts of the book described more proximate contexts for each role: the case studies focused mainly on what users do while the section on running an online service focused mainly on what information professionals do. Essentially, these chapters have brought together issues and contexts of practice, need and services as illustrated in Figure 25.1. The details of such diagrams are, of course, debatable, but the overall picture, with 'learning' at the centre of the interaction between the user and the information professional, is certainly a clear lesson from previous chapters. Many contexts are likely to be shared between the information professional and the user (indeed, as the case study with Jeremy illustrates nicely, these may be different roles played by the same person). For example, both are likely to need a solid knowledge of the subject or sector in which they are working, even though how they use this knowledge may differ. Similarly, the organisational context may well be shared, so that if work gets done in multidisciplinary teams, then that will affect how both information users and services work together. The organisational contexts and pressures for users will impact on the demands made on information

Figure 25.1 From practice to need, from need to service

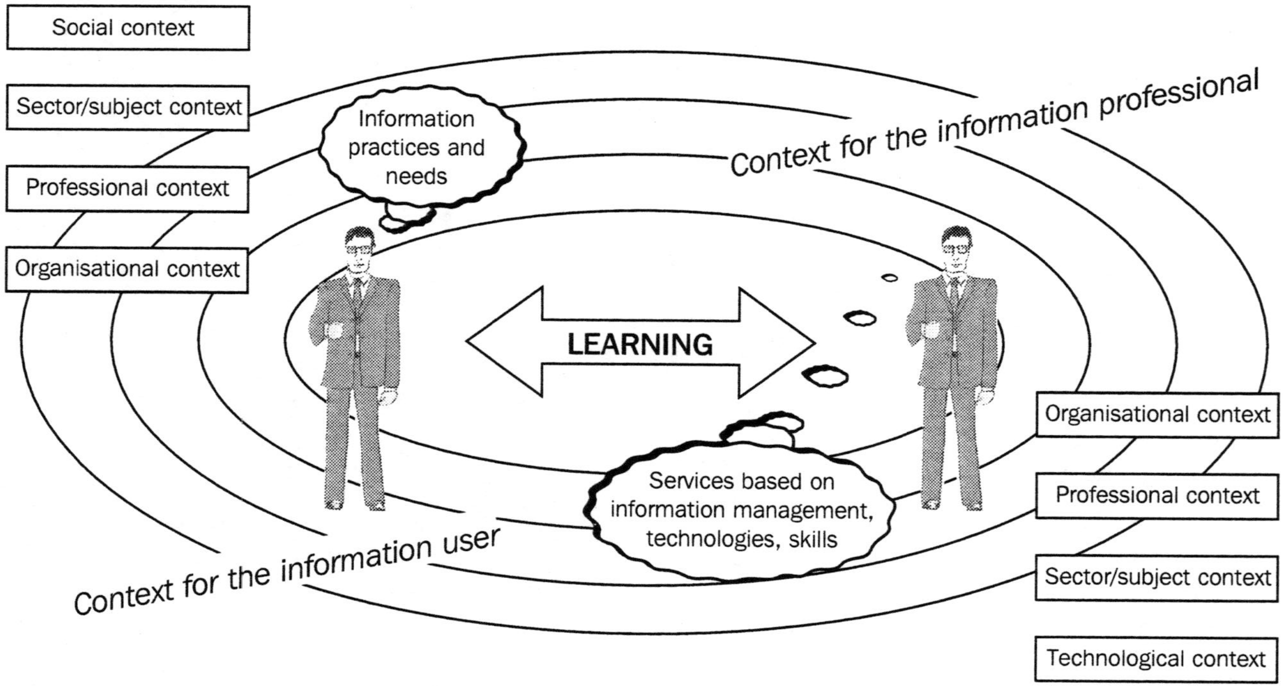

services, just as organisational strategic priorities and resources will affect service provision and access to information and services for those users. Figure 25.1 suggests that the social context (discussed in Chapter 23) is more relevant to users and that the technological context (discussed in Chapter 24) is more relevant to information professionals, although if this is true at all it is only likely to be so at a very broad level.

Learning

Figure 25.1 puts 'learning' at the heart of the interaction between users and information professionals, but what do we mean by 'learning' in this context? The notion that organisations need to acquire, manage and use knowledge in order to develop and maintain a competitive edge (however that is measured) is not new. The concept of the 'learning organisation' has its origins in the self-development movement of the 1970s, but the focus has moved gradually from the self-developing individual to the self-developing organisation. Michael Fullan (Gitlin, 2000) is one of the key proponents of the learning organisation in education. He argues that '...the key to development and change is finding ways to acquire new and better knowledge, to create a type of learning community'. A learning community of information users and providers is key to the success of an organisation.

If we focus on the inner portion of Figure 25.1, the essence of the learning organisation is to capture, share and facilitate the learning that is naturally occurring in the organisation and could be supported by what we now call knowledge management. The difference here is that organisations should learn from information and knowledge: the emphasis is not so much on whether information is appropriately stored and accessible, but on its origins, on what individuals and groups do with that knowledge (which decisions, which policies are made, what actions are taken) and on the contribution their outcomes make to the overall success of the organisation. Flexibility and adaptability are seen as key to successful learning organisations, with lean management and operational systems and processes supported by regular cycles of review. This implies two things. First, users need high-level and regularly updated information skills in order to learn effectively. Second, information services and systems need to offer fast access to relevant and contextualised information and they too need regularly to review the ways they operate.

If we now focus on the outer portion of Figure 25.1, learning organisations do not, themselves, operate and develop in isolation. They learn from others as well as from their own internal resources. External environments, contexts, systems and pressures all impact on the nature and content of the knowledge and information needed by organisations at any one time, and how they react and adapt to it. Information professionals and users within an organisation therefore need to deal with information from other sources, local or global, to be able to recognise its relevance and importance and to process and present it in a local organisational or subject context. A decade ago, Fullan (1993) noted the potential impact on organisations of the fields in which they operate: '...learning organisations respect their environments ... [they] live with them interactively'. He suggested that organisations that seek help for internal problems from external solutions or agencies show signs of 'vitality' whereas those that profess to self-sufficiency are heading for a dead end. Networks – professional, physical, technical, information – provide one platform for such interactions. A key skill here would appear to be that of 'environmental scanning' of both internal and external environments.

Evidence from the case studies and the preceding two chapters suggests that there are yet broader contexts, such as changing working practices and rapid technological change. These are the background to the 'Google culture' of satisficing (see Chapter 12), to multitasking and 'continual partial attention' (see Chapter 24) and to a feeling that many information professionals have: that there is a tension between the need to engage with users directly and the need to make the relationship between the user and the information as transparent and intuitive as possible. What can the response of the information professional be?

The changing role of the information professional

To answer this question, we need to look in more detail at how the learning interaction at the heart of Figure 25.1 may be structured. The right-hand side of Figure 25.2 describes 'what's behind the scenes' of an information service, and this needs increasingly to be modular, so that the different elements can be brought together in different combinations to suit different circumstances. In the online world, technologies and standards are emerging to allow this level of interoperability to happen not merely at the syntactic level but also at the semantic level (Dempsey, 2003). There are two roles here for information professionals: first to be involved in the production of reusable packages and interoperability standards; and second, to provide a service by using these tools. Whether you see yourself as a developer or a service provider, it is important to at least be familiar with (and preferably involved in) the work of the other.

Figure 25.2 shows three possible models (1–3) for the learning interaction at the heart of Figure 25.1, and you can certainly imagine others. A first role for the information professional running an online service is to judge the context and decide which model to adopt on any particular occasion.

The first model is familiar, where user needs are predictable (at least, broadly) because the user's organisational or professional context is stable. The legal profession might be an example here, where the job of lawyers remains basically the same as it has always been and, although new types of information source emerge over time, these do not profoundly disrupt the situation. Here we find information professionals of a familiar kind, contributing to their organisations by creating services, disseminating skills and good practice and increasingly supporting organisational learning by offering ways for users to share knowledge. Here is the gardener in the information ecology, tending the garden, encouraging good information practices and weeding out sources of misinformation.

The second model may be less familiar. The term 'barefoot librarian' was used in research by David Zeitlyn and others

Figure 25.2 Models of online information provision

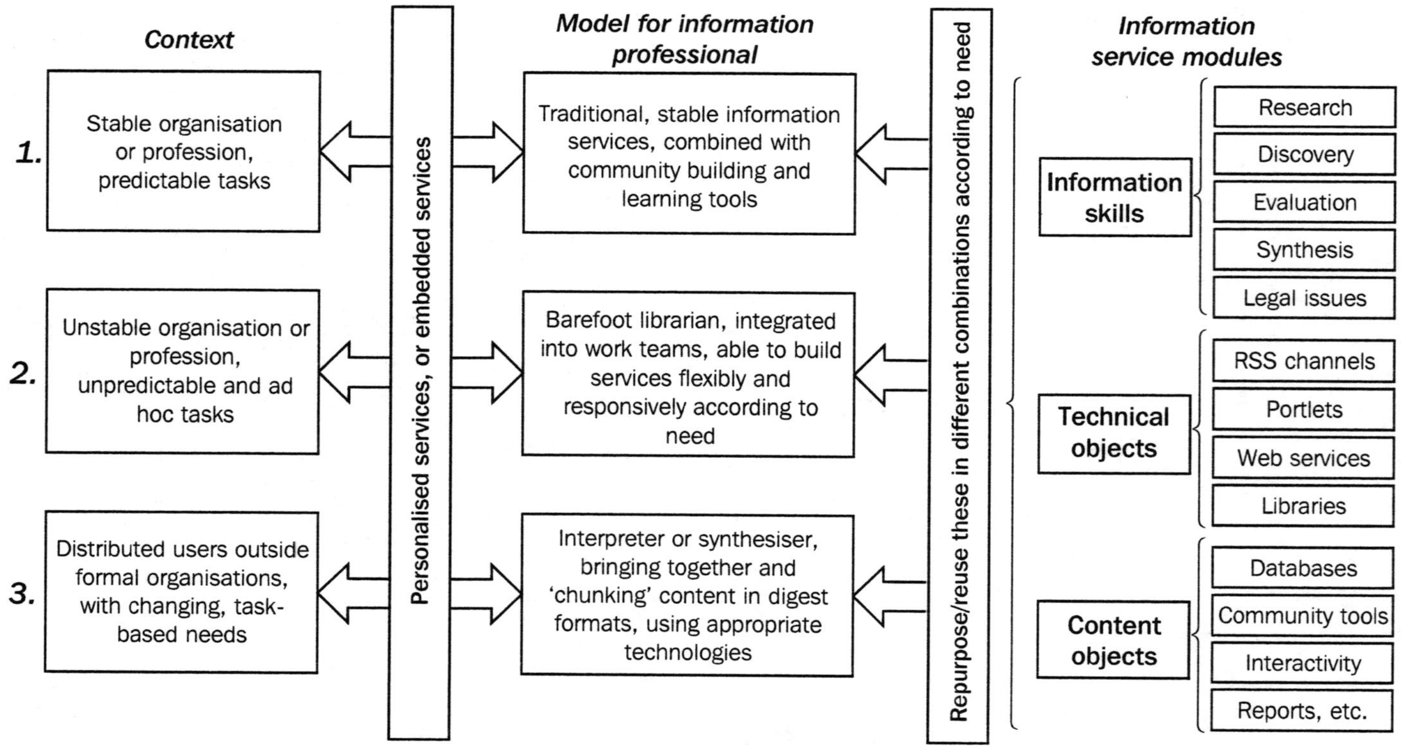

(Zeitlyn, David and Bex, 1999). David Zeitlyn, being an anthropologist, had come across the term 'barefoot doctor' in his work in Cameroon, where medical professionals worked in the field as a part of the community they served, with no fixed surgery or hospital. Recent trends in organisational working practices have emphasised mobile, multidisciplinary, multi-competence, task-based teams, and in this context the barefoot librarian becomes an appropriate role. Working as a part of the team – building services and resources as they are needed for as long as they are needed from the modular resources on the right edge of Figure 25.2 – the barefoot librarian is a mobile professional supporting mobile teams. The key part of this role is ensuring that the team can effectively learn both internally and from external sources.

The third model in Figure 25.2 is, at present, the preserve of a very few specialists who have managed to combine high-level information skills, familiarity with online tools and a wide, current knowledge of a particular subject area. Jeremy (Chapter 6) is perhaps the closest to an example among the case studies. Here, the product is not only an information service as such, but also some value-added work on the content such as synthesis or comment. In the Google culture, where users' attention is a scarce resource, information increasingly needs to be in the form of digests, processed to make it useful. This may mean that the service provided includes not only content and learning tools, but also (for example) judgement about who the user should contact on a certain issue or about who would make an effective advisory panel for a particular project. Clearly, this is some way from the usual definition of an information professional, but there is a real demand for this kind of hybrid work and it is territory to which the information profession has some claim.

Concluding remarks

As in so much of life, this book is a balance between practical experience and reflection and, taking Marshall McLuhan's maxim that the medium is the message, this is certainly one approach to the information profession. The medium of this book is also, well, a book. The message here is the familiar one that online information is not all information, and that both different types of knowledge and different types of attention exist offline. The hybrid library may be a somewhat outdated concept, but if the idea of the paperless office is a myth (Sellen and Harper, 2001), then work to integrate and learn from online, paper and tacit knowledge continues in as many ways as there are users.

Links

Accessibility Bookmarklets: *http://www.508compliant.com/tools.htm*

AccountingWeb: *http://www.accountingweb.co.uk/*

ACRL: *http://www.ala.org/acrl/*

ADBS: *http://www.adbs.fr/site/*

Adiuri: *http://www.adiuri.com/*

Adobe PDF accessibility: *http://access.adobe.com*

AFL-CIO (American Federation of Labor and Congress of Industrial Organizations): *http://www.afl-cio.org/*

AGRIS: *http://www.fao.org/agris*

AGROVOC: *http://www.fao.org/agrovoc/*

AlltheWeb: *http://www.alltheweb.com/*

AltaVista: *http://www.altavista.com/*

Amazon: *http://www.amazon.co.uk/*

Amazon Search Inside the Book: *http://www.amazon.com/exec/obidos/tg/browse/-/10197021/103-6875736-6797443*

American Psychological Association scheme: *http://www.apa.org/psycinfo/about/classcodes.html*

Apache: *http://www.apache.org/*

Arxiv: *http://xxx.lanl.gov/*

Ask: *http://www.ask.com/*

Athens: *http://www.athens.ac.uk/*

Autonomy: *http://www.autonomy.com/*

AVEL: *http://www.avel.edu.au/*

BBC: *http://www.bbc.co.uk/*

BBCi UK House Price Guide: *http://www.bbc.co.uk/homes/property/uk_price_guide/*

Berkeley Digital Library Copyright: *http://sunsite.berkeley.edu/Copyright/*

BETSIE text-only parser: *http://www.bbc.co.uk/education/betsie/index.html*

Big Blue Project: *http://www.leeds.ac.uk/bigblue/*

BIREME: *http://www.bireme.br/*

Biz/ed: *http://www.bized.ac.uk/*

Biz/ed Accessibility Statement: *http://www.bized.ac.uk/homeinfo/accessibility.htm*

Bluetooth: *http://www.bluetooth.com/*

Bobby Validator: *http://bobby.watchfire.com/bobby*

Bristol Biomed: *http://www.brisbio.ac.uk/*

Bristol Online Surveys (BOS): *http://www.survey.bris.ac.uk*

British Association of Adoption and Fostering: *http://www.baa.org.uk/*

British Library Catalogue: *http://blpc.bl.uk/*

Cambridge Scientific Abstracts: *http://md2.csa.com/csa/index.html*

CAROL (Company Annual Reports Online): *http://www.carol.co.uk/*

CAUL: *http://www.caul.edu.au/*

CCTR (Cochrane Controlled Trials Register): *http://www.cochrane.org/resources/brochure.htm#CCTR*

Center for Defense Information (CDI): *http://www.cdi.org/*

Cheshire: *http://cheshire.lib.berkeley.edu/*

Child Welfare League of America: *http://www.cwla.org/*

CINAHL Information Systems home: *http://www.cinahl.com/*

Cochrane Collaboration: *http://www.cochrane.org/index0.htm*

Cochrane Database of Systematic Reviews: *http://www.cochrane.org/reviews/index.htm*

Cochrane Library: *http://www.update-software.com/cochrane/*

Commission on Intellectual Property Rights: *http://www.iprcommission.org/*

Companies House UK: *http://www.companieshouse.gov.uk/info/*

Copyleft: *http://www.gnu.org/copyleft/copyleft.html*

Copyright Licensing Agency: *http://www.cla.co.uk/*

Council for the Central Laboratory of the Research Councils, Petabyte Data Storage: *http://www.e-science.clrc.ac.uk/Web/projects/petabyte*

Courrier International: *http://www.courrierinternational.com/*

Creating an accessibility statement: *http://diveintoaccessibility.org/day_30_creating_an_accessibility_statement.html*
Creative Commons: *http://creativecommons.org/*
Crystal Reports: *http://www.crystaldecisions.com/*
CSS Validator: *http://jigsaw.w3.org/css-validator/*
Data Documentation Initiative: *http://www.icpsr.umich.edu/DDI/*
DC.dot: *http://www.ukoln.ac.uk/metadata/dcdot/*
Department of Trade and Industry e-Science and Grid: *http://www.escience-grid.org.uk/*
Dewey Decimal Classification: *http://www.oclc.org/dewey/*
DigiLib2003, 'Towards a User-Centred Approach to Digital Libraries', 8–9 September 2003, Espoo, Finland: *http://www.lib.helsinki.fi/finelib/digilib/*
DMOZ Open Directory: *http://www.dmoz.org/*
Dublin Core: *http://dublincore.org/*
Dynamic Systems Development Method: *http://www.dsdm.com/*
Eblida ECUP: *http://www.eblida.org/ecup/*
ECDL2003: 7th European Conference on Research and Advanced Technology for Digital Libraries, 17–22 August 2003, Trondheim, Norway: *http://www.ecdl2003.org/*
Economic and Social Research Council: *http://www.esrc.ac.uk/*
Economic and Social Research Council Publication Scheme: *http://www.esrc.ac.uk/foi/index.htm*
Economist.com: *http://www.economist.co.uk/*
EMBASE: *http://www.embase.com/*
Encoded Archival Description: *http://www.loc.gov/ead/*
ENSSIB (Ecole Nationale Supérieure des Bibliothèques): *http://www.enssib.fr/*
ERIC: *http://www.eric.ed.gov/*
ETUC (European Trade Union Confederation): *http://www.etuc.org/*
European Commission: e-Accessibility: Web and People with Disabilities: *http://europa.eu.int/information_society/topics/citizens/accessibility/Web/index_en.htm*
European Science Foundation: *http://www.esf.org/*
European University Institute (EUI): *http://www.iue.it/*
Extreme Programming: *http://www.extremeprogramming.org/*
FAO (Food and Agriculture Organisation): *http://www.fao.org/*

FashionCapital: *http://www.fashioncapital.co.uk/*
Flash: *http://www.macromedia.com/software/flash/*
Free Pint: *http://www.freepint.com/*
FT: *http://www.ft.com/*
Global Reach: *http://www.glreach.com/globstats/*
Google: *http://www.google.com/*
Government Category List: *http://www.govtalk.gov.uk/schemasstandards/gcl.asp*
Groupement Français de l'Industrie de l'Information: *http:// www.gfii.asso.fr/*
Guardian Unlimited: *http://www.guardian.co.uk/*
H2G2: *http://www.bbc.co.uk/h2g2/guide/*
Haystack: *http://haystack.lcs.mit.edu/*
Health and Safety Executive: *http://www.hse.gov.uk/*
HistoryWired: *http://historywired.si.edu/index.html*
Homepage Reader: *http://www-3.ibm.com/able/hpr.html*
HTML Validator: *http://validator.w3.org/*
Human Factors International: *http://www.humanfactors.com/*
Humanities and Social Science Electronic Thesaurus: *http://www.data-archive.ac.uk/search/hassetSearch.asp*
IBM Technical Library: *http://www-106.ibm.com/developerworks/Web/library/*
IDS PayBenchMark: *http://www.idspaybenchmark.co.uk/*
IIS: *http://www.microsoft.com/WindowsServer2003/iis/*
iKeepBookmarks: *http://www.ikeepbookmarks.com/*
Income Data Services (IDS) Report: *http://www.incomesdata.co.uk/report/reportservice.htm*
INSEE (English version): *http://www.insee.fr/en/home/home_page.asp*
Institute of Development Studies: *http://www.ids.ac.uk/*
Institute of Electrical and Electronics Engineers: *http://www.ieee.org/*
Intellectual Property Rights Helpdesk: *http://www.cordis.lu/ipr-helpdesk/en/home.html*
Investors in People: *http://www.iipuk.co.uk/IIP/Internet/default.htm*
IRS Employment Review: *http://www.irsemploymentreview.com/*
Janet: *http://www.janet.ac.uk/*

Java: *http://java.sun.com/* or *http://java.com/* or *http://www.java.net/*

JISC: *http://www.jisc.ac.uk/*

JISC Information Environment: *http://www.jisc.ac.uk/index.cfm?name=ie_home*

JISC Legal Information Service: *http://www.jisc.ac.uk/legal*

Keeping Legal: *http://www.keepinglegal.com/*

Keeping Legal – Copyright: *http://www.keepinglegal.com/copyright%20site%20map.htm*

Labour Research Department: *http://www.lrd.org.uk/*

Le Monde: *http://www.lemonde.fr/*

LearnDirect (at UfI): *http://www.learningdirect.org/*

Learning and Skills Council (LSC): *http://www.lsc.gov.uk/*

Lessig Blog: *http://www.lessig.org/blog/*

Libraries and Archives Copyright Alliance: *http://www.cilip.org.uk/committees/laca/laca.html*

Library of Congress Classification Scheme: *http://www.loc.gov/catdir/cpso/lcco/lcco.html*

Library of Congress Subject Headings: *http://lcweb.loc.gov/catdir/cpso/cpso.html#subjects*

Linkpopularity.com: *http://www.linkpopularity.com/*

Linux: *http://www.linux.org/*

Lynx Browser: *http://ugweb.cs.ualberta.ca/~gerald/lynx-me.cgi*

Metadata Glossary: *http://www.ukoln.ac.uk/metadata/glossary/*

Mobile Bristol: *http://www.mobilebristol.co.uk/*

Mono: *http://www.go-mono.com/*

MySQL: *http://www.mysql.com/*

MyYahoo: *http://my.yahoo.com/*

NACVS (National Association of Councils for Voluntary Service): *http://www.nacvs.org.uk/*

National Cancer Institute Guidelines: *http://www.usability.gov/guidelines/index.html*

National Cancer Institute Usability: *http://www.usability.gov/*

National Electronic Library for Health(NeLH) (Cochrane access): *http://www.nelh.nhs.uk/cochrane.asp*

National Grid for Learning: *http://www.ngfl.gov.uk/*

National Learning Network (NLN): *http://www.nln.ac.uk/*

National Research Register: *http://www.update-software.com/national/*

NCVO (National Council for Voluntary Organisations): *http://www.ncvo-vol.org.uk/*

.Net: *http://www.microsoft.com/net/*

New Opportunities Fund Digitisation Programme: *http://www.nof-digitise.org/*

NewStart: *http://www.newstartmag.co.uk/*

NHS Centre for Reviews and Dissemination: *http://www.york.ac.uk/inst/crd/*

OAI-PMH: *http://www.openarchives.org/*

Online Information: *http://www.online-information.co.uk/*

Open Archives Initiative: *http://www.openarchives.org*

Open Source: *http://www.opensource.org/*

Oracle: *http://www.oracle.com/*

O'Reilly: *http://www.oreilly.com/*

Organisation for Economic Cooperation and Development: *http://www.oecd.org/home/*

Ovid: *http://www.ovid.com/site/index.jsp*

Perl: *http://www.perl.org/* or *http://www.perl.com/*

PHP: *http://www.php.net/*

Plone: *http://plone.org/*

PostgreSQL: *http://www.postgresql.org/*

PRINCE2: *http://www.prince2.org.uk/*

PsychInfo: *http://www.apa.org/psycinfo/*

Public Records Office Records Management: *http://www.pro.gov.uk/recordsmanagement/access/default.htm*

PubMed: *http://www.ncbi.nlm.nih.gov/entrez/query.fcgi*

Python: *http://www.python.org/*

Regard: *http://www.regard.ac.uk/*

Regard Data Protection Statement: *http://www.regard.ac.uk/regard/dpstatement*

Regeneration and Renewal: *http://www.regenerationmagazine.com/*

Resources for Economists on the Internet: *http://rfe.org/*

RevealingThings: *http://www.si.edu/revealingthings/*

RIME: *http://www4.ccip.fr/_rime/*

RoMEO: *http://www.lboro.ac.uk/departments/dis/disresearch/romeo/*
RSS: *http://www.w3.org/2001/10/glance/doc/howto#rss*
SCONUL: *http://www.sconul.ac.uk/*
Search Engine Watch: *http://searchenginewatch.com/webmasters/*
Selfpromotion.com: *http://www.selfpromotion.com/*
SHERPA: *http://www.sherpa.ac.uk/*
Sofa Project: *http://www.sofaproject.org.uk/sofa_main2.swf*
SOSIG (Social Science Information Gateway): *http://www.sosig.ac.uk/*
SOSIG Privacy Statement: *http://www.sosig.ac.uk/help/privacy.html*
SQL Server: *http://www.microsoft.com/sql/*
Subject Portals Project: *http://www.portal.ac.uk/spp/*
Sun Microsystems: *http://www.sun.com/*
TASI: *http://www.tasi.ac.uk/*
TASI Searching for and Retrieving Digital Images: *http://www.tasi.ac.uk/advice/using/srchandret.html*
TechDis: *http://www.techdis.ac.uk/*
UfI (University for Industry): *http://www.learningdirect.org/*
UK Data Archive: *http://www.data-archive.ac.uk/*
UK Evaluation Society: *http://www.evaluation.org.uk/*
UK LOM Core: *http://www.cetis.ac.uk/profiles/uklomcore*
UK Ministry of Defence Publication Scheme: *http://www.foi.mod.uk/*
UK National Statistics: *http://www.statistics.gov.uk/*
UK Office of the e-Envoy Web Guidelines: *http://www.e-envoy.gov.uk/Resources/WebGuidelines/fs/en*
UK Public Health Laboratory Service: *http://www.phls.co.uk/*
UKOLN: *http://www.ukoln.ac.uk/*
UN (United Nations): *http://www.un.org/*
Universal Decimal Classification: *http://www.udcc.org/*
University of Tarbes Journal Review: *http://www.iut-tarbes.fr/enquete/*
URFIST: *http://Web.ccr.jussieu.fr/urfist/*
US Department of Justice Computer Crime and Intellectual Property Section: *http://www.usdoj.gov/criminal/cybercrime/ip.html*

US Small Business Administration: *http://www.sba.gov/*

Usability Sciences Corporation Usability Test Video Clip: *http://www.usabilitysciences.com/corp/media/sample_test.htm*

User Interface Engineering: *http://www.uie.com/*

USMARC: *http://www.loc.gov/marc/*

Virtual Training Suite: *http://www.vts.rdn.ac.uk/*

VisCheck: *http://www.vischeck.com/vischeck/vischeckURL.php*

VolResource: *http://www.volresource.org.uk/index.htm*

Voscur: *http://www.voscur.org/home/index.shtml*

W3C (World Wide Web Consortium): *http://www.w3.org/*

W3C Alternative Web Browsers: *http://www.w3.org/WAI/References/Browsing*

W3C Cascading Style Sheets Homepage: *http://www.w3.org/Style/CSS/*

W3C Evaluation Tools: *http://www.w3.org/WAI/ER/existingtools.html*

W3C MarkUp Validation Service: *http://validator.w3.org/*

W3C OWL Web Ontology Language Overview: *http://www.w3.org/TR/owl-features/*

W3C Semantic Web: *http://www.w3.org/2001/sw/*

W3C WAI Checklist of Checkpoints for Authoring Tool Accessibility Guidelines 1.0: *http://www.w3.org/TR/WAI-AUTOOLS/atag10-chktable.html*

W3C WAI Checklist of Checkpoints for Web Content Accessibility Guidelines 1.0: *http://www.w3.org/TR/WCAG10/full-checklist.html*

W3C WAI Developing Organizational Policies on Web Accessibility: *http://www.w3.org/WAI/EO/Drafts/impl/pol.html*

W3C Web Accessibility Initiative: *http://www.w3.org/WAI/*

W3C Web Services Activity: *http://www.w3.org/2002/ws/.*

WAICENT (World Agricultural Information Center): *http://www.fao.org/waicent/*

Wanadoo: *http://www.wanadoo.fr/*

Watchfire WebXact: *http://www.webxact.com/*

WebTrends: *http://www.netiq.com/webtrends/default.asp*

WHO (World Health Organisation): *http://www.who.int/en/*

Wikipedia: *http://en.wikipedia.org/*

World Intellectual Property Organisation: *http://www.wipo.org/*

XML (eXtensible Markup Language): *http://www.w3.org/XML/*
Yahoo: *http://www.yahoo.com/*
Z39.50: *http://lcweb.loc.gov/z3950/agency/*
Zebra: *http://www.indexdata.dk/zebra/*
Zetoc: *http://zetoc.mimas.ac.uk/*
ZOPE: *http://www.zope.com/*

References

ACRL (2000) *Information Literacy Competency Standards for Higher Education*. Chicago: Association of College and Research Libraries. Available at: *http://www.ala.org/acrl/ilintro.html visited 19/12/2000.*

BBC (2000) 'Blair's five-year Internet pledge'. Available at: *http://news.bbc.co.uk/1/hi/uk/668795.stm.*

Bedwell, K. (2001) 'Thinking as a marketeer', *ASSIGNation: ASLIB Social Sciences Information Group and Network Journal*, 18 (4): 2–5.

Bell, D. (1974) *The Coming of Post-Industrial Society: A Venture in Social Forecasting*. London: Heinemann Educational.

Bennett, G. (2003) *Instant Messaging, with New Tools from Microsoft, AOL and the Rest*. Available at: *http://thetechnozone.com/pcbuyersguide/solutions/Web/instant_messaging.html.*

Bergman, M. (2001) 'The Deep Web: surfacing hidden value', *Journal of Electronic Publishing*, 7 (1). Available at: *http://www.press.umich.edu/jep/07-01/bergman.html.*

Blood, R. (2000) 'Weblogs: a history and perspective', taken from her blog, *Rebecca's Pocket*, 7 September 2000. Available at: *http://www.rebeccablood.net/essays/weblog_history.html.*

Bowker, G.C. and Leigh Star, S. (1999) *Sorting Things Out: Classification and Its Consequences*. Cambridge, MA: MIT Press.

Brand, A. and Daly, F. (2003) *Metadata Demystified: A Guide for Publishers*. Hanover, PA: Sheridan Press/Bethesda, MD: NISO Press.

Braunstein, M. and Levine, E.H. (2000) *Deep Branding on the Internet: Applying Heat and Pressure Online to Ensure a Lasting Brand*. Rocklin, CA: Prima Publishing.

British Psychological Society (2000) *Code of Conduct, Ethical Principles and Guidelines*. Available at: *http://www.bps.org.uk/documents/Code.pdf*.

Brown, I. (2003) *Implementing the European Union Copyright Directive*. Foundation for Information Policy Research. Available at: *http://www.fipr.org/copyright/guide/*.

Bundy, A. (2001) *For a Clever Country: Information literacy diffusion in the 21st century*. Adelaide: University of South Australia. Available at: *http://www.library.unisa.edu.au/papers/clever.htm*.

Cantu, C. (1997) *Virtual Teams*. Center for the Study of Work Teams, University of North Texas. Available at: *http://www.workteams.unt.edu/reports/Cantu.html*.

Castells, M. (2000) *The Rise of the Network Society*, 2nd edn. Oxford: Blackwell.

Castells, M. and Kreisler, H. (2001) *Identity and Change in the Network Society*. Available at: *http://globetrotter.berkeley.edu/people/Castells/castells-con0.html*.

CAUL (2000) *Information Literacy Standards*, 1st edn. Canberra: Council of Australian University Librarians. Available at *http://www.caul.edu.au/*.

Chowdhury, G.C. and Chowdhury, S. (2003) *Introduction to Digital Libraries*. London: Facet.

Christensen, C.M. (1997) *The Innovator's Dilemma: When New Technologies Cause Great Firms to Fail*. Boston, MA: Harvard Business School Press.

Commission on Intellectual Property Rights (2002) *Final Report*. Available at: *http://www.iprcommission.org/graphic/documents/final_report.htm*.

Cooke, A. (2001) *A Guide to Finding Quality Information on the Internet: Selection and Evaluation Strategies*, 2nd edn. London: Library Association.

Cornish, W.R. and Llewelyn, D. (2003) *Intellectual Property: Patents, Copyright, Trade Marks and Allied Rights*, 5th edn. London: Sweet & Maxwell.

Davison, M.J. (2003) *The Legal Protection of Databases*. Cambridge: Cambridge University Press.

Day, M. (2001) 'Metadata in a nutshell', *Information Europe*, 6 (2): 11. Draft available at: *http://www.ukoln.ac.uk/metadata/publications/nutshell/*.

De Sáez, E.E. (2002) *Marketing Concepts for Libraries and Information Services*, 2nd edn. London: Facet.

Deegan, M. and Tanner, S. (2002) *Digital Futures: Strategies for the Information Age*. London: Library Association Publishing.

Delphi Group (2002) *Taxonomy and Content Classification*. Available at: *http://www.delphigroup.com/coverage/taxonomy.htm*.

Dempsey, L. (2003) 'The recombinant library: portals and people', *Journal of Library Administration* (forthcoming). Preprint available at: *http://www.oclc.org/research/staff/dempsey/dempsey_recombinant_library.pdf*.

Department for Education and Skills (2001) *Delivering Results: A Strategy for 2006*. DfES Publications. Available to download from: *http://www.dfes.gov.uk/delivering-results/*.

DESIRE (2000) *DESIRE Information Gateways Handbook*. Available at: *http://www.desire.org/handbook/*.

Doyle, C.S. (1992) *Outcome Measures for Information Literacy within the National Education Goals of 1990. Report to the National Forum on Information Literacy. Summary of Findings*. ED 351 033.

Dupuis, E.A. (1997) 'The inforamtion literacy challenge: addressing the changing needs of our students through our programs', *Internet Reference Services Quarterly*, 2(2/3): 93–111.

Eason, K., MacIntyre, R., Apps, A. and Ashby, M. (2003) *Early Integrators and the Passive Majority. An Evaluation of a Large Web-based Bibliographic Reference Database*. Conference presentation at DigiLib2003, Espoo, Finland. Available at: *http://www.lib.helsinki.fi/finelib/digilib/pp/eason.ppt*.

European Parliament and Council (2001) *Directive 2001/29/EC of the European Parliament and of the Council of 22 May 2001 on the harmonisation of certain aspects of copyright and related rights in the information society*. Available at: *http://europa.eu.int/eur-lex/pri/en/oj/dat/2001/l_167/l_16720010622en00100019.pdf*

Ferguson, B. (1998) *Subject Analysis*. Englewood, CO: Libraries Unlimited.

Fogg, B.J. (2002) *Stanford Guidelines for Web Credibility. A Research Summary from the Stanford Persuasive Technology Lab*. Stanford University. Available at: *http://www.webcredibility.org/guidelines/*.

Friedlein, A. (2001) *Web Project Management. Delivering Successful Commercial Web Sites*. San Fransisco: Morgan Kaufmann.

Friedman, T. (2001) 'Cyber-serfdom', *The New York Times on the Web*, 30 January. Available at: *http://www.nytimes.com/2001/01/30/opinion/30FRIE.html?ex=1072328400&en=eeeb2d787bf2792f&ei=5070*.

Fuccella, J., Pizzolato, J. and Franks, J. (1998) 'Web site user centered design: techniques for gathering requirements and tasks', *Internetworking*, June. Available at: *http://internettg.org/newsletter/june98/user_requirements.html*

Fullan, M.G. (1993) *Change Forces: Probing the Depths of Education Reform*. London: Falmer Press.

Gilliland-Swetland, A. (2000) 'Setting the stage', in M. Baca (ed.), *Introduction to Metadata: Pathways to Digital Information*. Los Angeles: The Getty. Available at: *http://www.getty.edu/research/conducting_research/standards/intrometadata/*.

Gitlin, A. (2000) 'The truth is in the details (review of Fullan, M. (1999): Change Forces: The Sequel. Philadelphia. Falmer Press)', *Journal of Education Change*, 1: 211–17.

Gorman, M. (2000) *From Card Catalogues to WebPACS*. Presentation at the Library of Congress Bicentennial Conference on Bibliographic Control for the New Millennium. Washington, DC, 15 November 2000. Available at: *http://www.loc.gov/catdir/bibcontrol/gorman_paper.html*.

Grayson, L. and Gomersall, A. (2003) *A Difficult Business: Finding the Evidence for Social Science Reviews*, Working Paper 19. London: ESRC UK Centre for Evidence Based Policy and Practice. Available at: *http://www.evidencenetwork.org/Documents/wp19.pdf*.

Greensmith, J. and Cayzer, S. (2003) *An Artificial Immune System Approach to Semantic Document Classification*. Available at:

http://www-uk.hpl.hp.com/people/steve_cayzer/papers/030901SemanticClassification.pdf.

Grimshaw, J. (2000) *How to Find Information – Social Sciences.* London: British Library.

Gupta, P. (2000) *Short Message Service: What, How and Where?* Available at: *http://www.wirelessdevnet.com/channels/sms/features/sms.html.*

Harnad, S. (2001) *For Whom the Gate Tolls? How and why to free the refereed research literature online through author/institution self-archiving, now.* Available at: *http://cogprints.soton.ac.uk/documents/disk0/00/00/16/39/index.html.*

HeadLine (1999) 'The HeadLine personal information environment', *Headline Newsletter*, Autumn. Available at: *http:// www.headline.ac.uk/public/diss/nl-pie.pdf.*

Heery, R. (2003) *Delivering HILT as a JISC IE Shared Service.* Available at: *http://www.ukoln.ac.uk/metadata/hilt/m2m-report/hilt-final-report.html.*

Heery, R., Powell, A. and Day, M. (1997) *Metadata.* London: Library Information Technology Centre.

Hudson, M. (1999) *Managing without Profit. The Art of Managing Third Sector Organisations.* Penguin: London.

Jackson, G., Kezar, A., Kozi, M. and de las Alas, N. (2000) *Preparing Scholarly Reviews of the Literature: A Webtorial.* Available at: *http://www.gwu.edu/~litrev/.*

Jacobs, N. and Huxley, L. (2002) 'From static content to dynamic communities: the evolution of networked educational resources', *Online Information Review*, 26 (1): 19–29.

Jenkins, C. and Morley, M. (eds.) (1999) *Collection Management in Academic Libraries*, 2nd edn. Aldershot: Gower.

Jones, S., Cunningham, S.J. and McNab, R. (1998) 'Usage analysis of a digital library', *Proceedings of the Third ACM Conference on Digital Libraries.* Available at: *http://www.cs.waikato.ac.nz/~nzdl/publications/1998/Jones-Cunningham-McNab-DL98.pdf.*

Jordan, P. and Lloyd, C. (2002) *Staff Management in Library and Information Work*, 4th edn. Aldershot: Ashgate.

Kakavelakis, I. and Macdonald, G. (2003) 'Cognitive-behavioural training interventions for assisting foster carers in the management of difficult behaviour (Protocol for a Cochrane Review)', *The Cochrane Library*, Issue 2. Oxford: Update Software.

Kupersmith, J. (2003) *Library Terms That Users Understand*. Available at: *http://www.jkup.net/terms.html*.

Learning and Teaching Portal Team (2003) *Learning and Teaching Portal Services Project Plan: Version 4*. Available at: *http://www.ltsn.ac.uk/embedded_object.asp?id=19096&prompt=yes&filename=LTP004*.

Lervik, J. (2003) *Digital Libraries: What should We Expect from Search Engines?* Conference presentation ECDL2003, Trondheim, Norway. Available at: *http://www.ecdl2003.org/presentations/invited/Lervik/Lervik.slides.pdf*.

Letourneau, C. (2003) *Accessible Web Design – A Definition*. Available from Starling Access Services site at: *http://www.starlingweb.com/webac.htm*.

Light, J. (2001) 'Rethinking the digital divide', *Harvard Educational Review*, 71 (4). Available at: *http://www.edreview.org/harvard01/2001/wi01/w01light.htm*.

Line, M. (2000) 'Social science information – the poor relation', *IFLA Journal*, 26 (3): 177–9.

Lipnack, J. and Stamps, J. (2000) *Virtual Teams: People Working Across with Technology*. New York: John Wiley & Sons.

Lyman, P. and Varian, H.R. (2003) *How Much Information*. Available at: *http://www.sims.berkeley.edu/how-much-info-2003*.

McCarthy, R. (2003) 'Salam's story', *Guardian Unlimited*, 30 May. Available at: *http://www.guardian.co.uk/g2/story/0,3604,966768,00.html*.

Macoustra, J. (2003) 'Information literacy in a corporate environment', *Free Pint*, no. 132. Available at: *http://www.freepint.com/issues/060303.pdf*.

Maguire, M. (1998) *User-Centred Requirements Handbook*. Available at: *http://www.ejeisa.com/nectar/respect/5.3/index.htm*.

Manning, H., McCarthy, J.C. and Souza, R.K. (1998) 'Why most web sites fail', *Interactive Technology Series*, 3 (7). Forrester Research.

Markey, K. (1984) 'Interindexer consistency tests: a literature review and report of a test of consistency in indexing visual materials', *Library and Information Science Research*, 6 (2), 155–77.

Martin, A. and Rader, H. (eds.) (2003) *Information and IT Literacy: Enabling Learning in the 21st Century*. London: Facet.

Mayo, A. and Lank, E. (1994) *The Power of Learning*. London: IPD.

Meadows, J. (1998) *Communicating Research*. London: Academic Press.

Nardi, B.A. and O'Day, V. (1999) *Information Ecologies: Using Technology with Heart*. London: MIT Press.

National Information Standards Organization (1993) *Guidelines for the Construction, Format, and Management of Monolingual Thesauri*. Available at: *http://www.techstreet.com/cgi-bin/detail?product_id=52601*.

Negnevitsky, M. (2002) *Artificial Intelligence: A Guide to Intelligent Systems*. New York: Addison Wesley.

Nielsen, J. (1994) *Ten Usability Heuristics*. Available at: *http://www.useit.com/papers/heuristic/heuristic_list.html*.

Nielsen, J. (1997) *Search and You May Find*. Available from: *http://www.useit.com/alertbox/9707b.html*.

Nielsen, J. (2000) *Why You Only Need to Test with 5 Users*. Available at: *http://www.useit.com/alertbox/20000319.html*.

Nielsen, J. (2003) *Usability 101*. Available at: *http://www.useit.com/alertbox/20030825.html*.

Nielsen, J., Schemenaur, P.J. and Fox, J. (2002) *Writing for the Web*. Available at: *http://www.sun.com/980713/webwriting/*.

Nutley, S. and Davies, H. (2000) 'Making a reality of evidence-based practice', in H.T.O. Davies, S.M. Nutley and P.C. Smith (eds), *What Works? Evidence-Based Policy and Practice in Public Services*. Bristol: Policy Press.

Office of the E-Envoy (2003) *Quality Framework for UK Government Web Site Design: Usability Issues for Government*

Web Sites. Available at: *http://www.e-envoy.gov.uk/assetRoot/04/00/37/39/04003739.pdf.*

Perrin, B. (2002) 'How to – and How Not to – Evaluate Innovation', *Evaluation*, 8 (1): 13–28.

Pinfield, S., Gardner, M. and MacColl, J. (2002) 'Setting up an institutional eprint archive', *Ariadne*, 31, March–April. Available at: *http://www.ariadne.ac.uk/issue31/eprint-archives/.*

Poster, M. (1990) *The Mode of Information: Poststructuralism and Social Context*. Cambridge: Polity Press in association with Basil Blackwell.

Pothen, P. (2003) *From Understanding User Behaviour to Transforming Delivery: The Experience of the UK*. Conference presentation DigiLib 2003, Espoo, Finland.

Prensky, M. (2001) 'Digital natives, digital immigrants', *On the Horizon*, 9 (5). Available at: *http://www.marcprensky.com/writing/.*

Rader, H.B. (1996) 'User education and information literacy for the next decade: an international perspective', *Reference Services Review*, 24(2): 71–6.

Ramsden, A. (2003) *Using Spreadsheets to Promote Student Understanding*. Available at: *http://www.bized.ac.uk/educators/he/spreadsheet/.*

Ronan, J. (2003) Chat Reference: A Guide to Live Virtual Reference Services. Westport, CT: Libraries Unlimited.

Rowley, J. (2001) *Information Marketing*. Aldershot: Ashgate.

Roy, M.C., Dewit, O. and Aubert, B.A. (2001) 'The impact of interface usability on trust in Web retailers', *Internet Research: Electronic Networking Applications and Policy*, 11 (5): 388–98.

SCONUL (1990) in Corrall, S. and Hathaway, H. (eds) (2000) *Seven Pillars of Wisdom? Good Practice in Information Skills Development: Conference Proceedings*. University of Warwick, 6–7 July 2000. London: SCONUL.

Sellen, A.J. and Harper, R.H.R. (2001) *The Myth of the Paperless Office*. Cambridge, MA: MIT Press.

SFEFC (2001) *Scottish Further Education Training Needs Analysis*. Available at: *http://www.rsc-ne-scotland.ac.uk/tna/execsumm.pdf.*

Shachtman, N. (2003) 'Pentagon alters LifeLog Project', *Wired News*, 14 July. Available at: *http://www.wired.com/news/politics/0,1283,59607,00.html.*

Snyder, C. (2001) *Paper Prototyping: Sure, it's low-tech, but this usability testing method can help you sidestep problems before you write your code.* Available from: *http://www-106.ibm.com/developerworks/library/us-paper/?n-us-1181.*

Special Libraries Association (1997) *Marketing Matters: An SLA Information Kit.* Washington, DC: Special Libraries Association.

Spool, J.M. (2002) *How Usability-Focused Companies Think.* Available at: *http://world.std.com/~uieweb/focused.htm.*

Spool, J., DeAngelo, T., Scanlon, T., Schroeder, W. and Snyder, C. (1999) *Web Site Usability.* San Fransisco: Morgan Kaufmann.

Stamatoudi, I.A. and Torremans, P.L.C. (eds) (2000) *Copyright in the New Digital Environment: The Need to Redesign Copyright.* London: Sweet & Maxwell.

Standish Group International Ltd (1994) *The CHAOS Report.* Available at: *http://www.standishgroup.com/sample_research/chaos_1994_2.php.*

Tenopir, C. et al. (2003) *Increasing Effective Student Use of the Scientific Journal Literature.* Available at: *http://Web.utk.edu/~tenopir/nsf/presentations.html.*

Thompson, B. (2003) 'Copyright defender advises Number 10', *BBC News.* Available at: *http://news.bbc.co.uk/1/hi/technology/2743961.stm.*

Thoreau, H.D. (1965 [1854]) *Walden; or, Life in the Woods.* Harper & Row.

UK government (1988) *Copyright, Designs and Patents Act.* Available at: *http://www.hmso.gov.uk/acts/acts1988/Ukpga_19880048_en_1.htm.*

UK government (1995) *Disability Discrimination Act.* Available at: *http://www.hmso.gov.uk/acts/acts1995/1995050.htm.*

UK government (1998) *Data Protection Act.* Available at: *http://www.hmso.gov.uk/acts/acts1998/19980029.htm.*

UK government (2000) *Freedom of Information Act.* Available at: *http://www.hmso.gov.uk/acts/acts2000/20000036.htm.*

UK government (2001) *Special Educational Needs and Disability Act*. Available at: *http://www.hmso.gov.uk/acts/acts2001/20010010.htm*.

US government (1998) *Digital Millennium Copyright Act*. Overview available at: *http://www.loc.gov/copyright/legislation/dmca.pdf*.

VPN Consortium (2003) *VPN Technologies: Definitions and Requirements*. Available at: *http://www.vpnc.org/vpn-technologies.html*.

W3C (1997) *Intellectual Property Rights Overview*. Available at: *http://www.w3.org/IPR/*.

Warschauer, M. (2002) 'Reconceptualising the digital divide', *First Monday*, 7 (7). Available at: *http://www.firstmonday.dk/issues/issue7_7/warschauer/*.

WIPO (1996) *WIPO Copyright Treaty*. Available at: *http://www.wipo.org/clea/docs/en/wo/wo033en.htm*.

Wood, S. (2003) 'UK Freedom of Information Act 2000: the road to implementation', *Free Pint*, 136, 1 May. Available at: *http://www.freepint.com/issues/010503.pdf*.

Woolgar, S. (2002) *Virtual Society? Technology, Cyberbole, Reality*. Oxford: Oxford University Press.

Zeitlyn, D., David, M. and Bex, J. (1999) *Knowledge Lost in Information: Patterns and Non-use of Networked Bibliographic Resources*. Office for Humanities Communication, Publication 11.

Index

Printed in the United States
19734LVS00001B/5